T0283323

The BOOK OF SHADOW WORK

ALSO BY KEILA SHAHEEN

The Shadow Work Journal

The Vibrational Poetry Book

The Lucky Girl Journal

The 369 Journal

The BOOK OF SHADOW WORK

Unlock the True You: The Must-Have Guide to Inner Healing and Authenticity

KEILA SHAHEEN

PRIMERO SUEÑO PRESS

ATRIA

New York Amsterdam/Antwerp London Toronto Sydney New Delhi

This publication is intended to provide helpful and informative material on the subject addressed. It is sold with the understanding that the author and publisher are not engaged in rendering mental health, medical, or any other kind of personal or professional services in the book. The author and publisher specifically disclaim all responsibility for any liability, loss or risk, personal or otherwise, which is incurred as a consequence, directly or indirectly, of the use or application of any of the contents of this book.

Some names and identifying characteristics have been changed.

Internet addresses and QR codes given in the book were accurate at the time it went to press. The author and publisher are not responsible for changes to third-party websites.

PRIMERO SUEÑO PRESS

ATRIA

An Imprint of Simon & Schuster, LLC
1230 Avenue of the Americas
New York, NY 10020

First Primero Sueño Press/Atria Books hardcover edition January 2025

PRIMERO SUEÑO PRESS / ATRIA BOOKS and colophon are trademarks of Simon & Schuster, LLC

For information about special discounts for bulk purchases, please contact Simon & Schuster Special Sales at 1-866-506-1949 or business@simonandschuster.com.

The Simon & Schuster Speakers Bureau can bring authors to your live event. For more information or to book an event, contact the Simon & Schuster Speakers Bureau at 1-866-248-3049 or visit our website at www.simonspeakers.com.

Interior design by Kris Tobiassen

Manufactured in the United States of America

1 3 5 7 9 10 8 6 4 2

ISBN 978-1-6680-6994-3
ISBN 978-1-6680-6995-0 (ebook)

CONTENTS

INTRODUCTION

HOW I GOT HERE

I live in a funky old house with my husband in Austin, Texas. Most days I spend cooped up in my little office upstairs, where the heater hums year-round. Surrounded by paintings, sheet music, and books that contain what I believe to be the greatest secrets of the universe, here is where I hold space for all parts of myself: the good, the sad, the optimistic, the angry. Here I am the creator, the doer, the thinker, the dreamer.

This is also the place where I ask myself hard questions, like "How did I get here?" Some days I know right away. Some days I need to be reminded, and so gravity pulls me down to the floor, where I am eye level with the stacks of my past journals. My current self needs to hear from my past self. Seeing where I came from, recognizing where I've gotten to, has a way of making me grateful and inspiring me to dream of more. It is a prelude that leads me to ask myself, "Where am I going next?"

As I write this, I'm reading an entry in one of my old journals, when I was twenty-two. In it, I proclaim (yes, in all caps): "I'VE EXPERIENCED THE SMALLNESS AND THE GRANDNESS, THE POWER AND THE POWERLESSNESS, THE LIVELINESS AND THE LIFELESSNESS. ALL TO HAVE CLARITY. I CAME

HERE TO KNOW WHAT MY PURPOSE IS IN THIS LIFETIME. I FEEL SOMETHING INSIDE OF ME SO BIG. I CAN'T EVEN SEE IT, BUT I CAN FEEL IT. IT CAN CHANGE THE WORLD."

I penned those words shortly after coming out of a depressive episode, a period when I contemplated my purpose on earth, questioned the callousness of the world, and wondered if, or when, I would ever get my spark back.

Have you ever felt as if the very essence of your being has been dimmed? As if you were a ghost and everyone else was real? The days come and go, and you're stuck in a loop of repetition leading nowhere, concerned only by survival. The thought of restarting each morning is a disappointment.

Have you ever felt as if the very essence of your being has been dimmed? As if you were a ghost and everyone else was real? The days come and go, and you're stuck in a loop of repetition leading nowhere, concerned only by survival. The thought of restarting each morning is a disappointment.

In a loop like this, one disappointment leads to another, and the expectation of less and worse reinforces itself. Loops build momentum over time, and they can go on forever if you don't do something to intervene. The deeper the loop, the less control you have over it, and the more control it has over you. In Buddhism this is called *samskara*. Samskaras are habits, patterns, or mental scars we form through repeated experiences.

Reminder to affirm: I am not the sum of my habits, but the consciousness observing them.

When you are suffering from deeply ingrained samskaras, rooted in long-past childhood experiences, how your life looks on the surface might not correlate with the intensity of your emotions. That dissonance can make you feel even further misunderstood, like you're living a dual existence.

That was the case for me. Nothing happening in my life seemed to justify my suffering, so I also felt guilty for feeling bad. From the outside, everything looked exciting and on track: after getting married, I moved from Houston to Austin for a new job at a tech company. I was excited at first, but soon that excitement turned into anxiety and fear of failure. What I thought was my big break felt more like a big mistake. In meetings, the stage fright that haunted me when I was little came back, and I couldn't speak up. The corporate lingo was confusing, and I wasn't even sure what my job was supposed to be.

I felt small, weak, and like a failure, just as I used to in school. Back then, I wasn't part of any clique, and the subtle bullying and judgment weighed on me. Every bad grade felt like a punch in the gut, especially when I was trying my hardest. All those feelings came rushing back in this digital playground of a corporate workplace.

I also started feeling like something important was missing—like I wasn't following my true calling, even though I didn't know what it was. The real me felt hidden deep down inside, far away, and I wanted to free her. I had to. I just didn't have a clue how to go about it.

The hardest part was when my husband would ask me what was wrong, and I had no idea how to explain myself. I felt a wave of relief to be asked, finally, after pretending to be okay for so long. But I felt suffocated as my emotions pressed heavily against me. Silence settled into the air instead, leaving gaps and disconnects when usually our conversation flowed easily. Then I'd have an emotional breakdown, with a rush of tears and confusing fragments of half thoughts I had to force out of myself.

No matter who you are, it takes tremendous courage to admit your struggles. It's even harder when you're used to putting everyone else's struggles above your own. Growing up with my parents and my brother, I was used to being the strong one. I had to keep it together for them. I was the peacemaker, the mediator, the source of sanity when emotional turmoil arose. Opening up and letting someone else help me, even my husband, the person who really cared, was almost impossible.

No matter who you are, it takes tremendous courage to admit your struggles.

When you're on the outside looking in, everything seems clear. But when you're on the inside trying to look further in, it's often dark and confusing, like trying to see your reflection without a mirror. That's why it's so much easier to help a friend out, and it's much harder to do the same for yourself.

I finally found the courage to seek help. The pandemic was raging, so I approached the Zoom session I had booked with a therapist with hope and excitement. From her profile, she seemed like she could really understand someone like me: introverted, intense, sensitive, with a strong sense of justice. (I am a Myers-Briggs INFJ, if that means anything to you.) But then the universe decided to add a twist to my story. Technical glitches kept me stranded outside the virtual meeting room for the first five minutes. That delay was too much for the therapist, who cut me off, reacting without any understanding. She sent me an email, brimming with frustration, expressing her disappointment over my delay and concluding that we weren't a good fit.

I wasn't in a great state for that. It felt like the universe was serving me up even more of the isolation and misunderstanding I was struggling to escape. I was finally ready to open up, and yet the world seemed to turn its back, leaving me with so many unanswered questions and a heavy heart.

Sometimes starting once isn't enough. You have to get knocked down some more times before things start to look up. It takes a few forceful interventions to stop the loop's momentum before you can break out and begin to move in a new direction.

Pain is the breaker. Pain creates the friction needed for real change to happen. It's a crucial part of the story. Don't give up on yourself in the face of pain.

Pain is the breaker. Pain creates the friction needed for real change to happen. It's a crucial part of the story. Don't give up on yourself in the face of pain.

My sadness started turning into anger. We live in a world that is terrified of women's anger, but I assure you that it can be an exquisite catalyst. I was angry because I wasn't getting over feeling cast aside, lost, and unaccepting of myself. I also knew I didn't want to get used to that feeling of being adrift and self-hating.

Sometimes anger is beautiful, transformative. The anger of when you've had enough. The anger that makes you set boundaries. The anger that transforms passivity into change. This anger signals that you are ready for more.

As it went from a simmer to a boil, my anger at myself and at the world turned into passion and fire. I decided I would just go find myself on my own, whatever it took. I was raised in a primarily Catholic household, which laid the foundation for my belief in a loving, omnipresent God. However, deep inside my being, I held a more universal understanding of this divine love. I began waking up at the ungodly hour of 4 a.m. to read and study works of spirituality and self-help, meditate, and do yoga. I looked for new techniques and insights into how I could transcend my pain by engaging with it, not trying to escape it or wish it away.

Somehow, even then, I knew that facing it all was key. Somehow I approached myself with reverence and compassion and gave space to the emotional storms I was still going through. It was as if a light had turned on in the darkness, showing me the way forward. I held my chest to feel my heartbeat, and I remembered that I was connected to all that is. I remembered, too, that I was the driver of my life. I realized that I could soar, despite my trauma, my conditioning, my anxieties. I understood that the way to all that was within me, not outside me.

I started to ask myself questions and listened with an open heart and an open mind to what came back. When I felt triggered by something or someone, instead of instantly reacting to the trigger, I would slow down and ask myself, "What would someone who truly loved themselves do right now? What would my highest self do?"

The answer I got was to journal.

So I started to pour out my fears into notebooks, unraveling them to understand their roots. Soon the process was not simply writing, it was transferring the weight of my emotions from the depths of my being onto the lightness of paper. It was a physical and symbolic act of separation, a way of disentangling myself from my convoluted feelings inside and making sense of them. It was more than mere reflection; it felt like an energetic cleansing, a healing.

Amid this cathartic process, I kept poking around online, and in books, for spiritual and therapeutic information wherever I could find it. During one long session in front of the computer, I stumbled upon the term "shadow work," and the writings of the Swiss psychoanalyst Carl Gustav Jung.

Shadow work sounded elusive and dark, but also like it might be a missing piece of a puzzle. Something in me responded to it instinctively. I'm glad I paid attention.

Jung was a therapist and thought leader who helped define the modern notion of the human psyche. Even though he spent a lot of his time studying and treating human pain and dysfunction, he saw people as inherently sovereign and powerful. For his inquisitive, spiritual bent—he was fascinated by shamans, astrology, and the *I Ching* and frequently discussed the human soul—some consider Jung the father of the New Age movement, too. He took a poetic, broad-minded approach to people and their problems and was vexed by the developing modern era for how it thwarted a more genuine experience of individuality. He wasn't afraid to dive into and write about his own personal life either, which I find incredibly brave given the premium his profession put on dry objectivity and holding oneself as the ultimate authority.

A prolific writer, Jung expressed himself with complexity and nuance, which can make some of his vast body of work challenging to read. But I have found it a pleasure anyway, to experience the hope and frustration in his voice, which comes through clearly and often.

Jung was the person to conceive of and define the shadow as an unconscious aspect of our personality that we don't readily see in ourselves but that is integral to our whole being. It's the part of ourselves we repress from our conscious waking life, because we, or society, don't approve.

The idea that to be whole I needed my shadow too intrigued me. Shadow work, or the act of confronting and embracing the shadow in a spirit of openness, curiosity, and acceptance, wasn't just about managing or taming the parts of myself I wanted to deny or that I disliked. It was about achieving a fuller understanding of who I was, including my potential strengths and points of genius that I might have hidden from myself too. That *really* appealed to me.

Jung described the shadow as always there, trailing quietly behind you, and evolving alongside you as you grow and mature. It's in every personal joke you tell, every overthought decision, every unexplained mood swing, every impulse drink or text, and every quick overreaction, every envious or jealous moment, every romantic projection. It's this subtle part of you—influencing, but not often enough acknowledged—that you can't transform unless you face it and feel it. Isn't it ironic that to truly heal, you must first fully feel?

Jung's mainframe emphasized integrating our fragmented selves into a more cohesive, honest, and powerfully genuine whole through contact with and the acceptance of our shadows. It's not a question of escaping your shadow or making it go away, but simply loving it as a part of you. This felt to me like the way out of a prison of self-hate and into one part of the purpose I had been missing. I would do this, I said to myself. I set myself the challenge.

As I immersed myself in Jung's works, I recognized in him a fellow seeker with a valuable perspective on just how enormous and special humanity is. For all his worry about how society was evolving—away from nature and instinct, over-reliant on machines—he never gave up on our potential. As someone who has also had premonition dreams and who possesses a vivid imagination and deep curiosity about herself, Jung's work spoke to me on a profound level. The more I delved into his theories, the more I uncovered about the intricate layers of my own mind. It felt like having a conversation with my soul.

Jung defined the self and society as bound up together, even if they sometimes seem to be working at cross purposes. Though Jung believed that change always had to start with oneself, he also said that facing and integrating the shadow isn't something we do just for ourselves, but for the whole world and the future.

Any journey into shadow work is not about getting lost in the darkness but about illuminating it, accepting it, and, in the process, transforming what you find into a source of strength and self-awareness.

I started doing shadow work in my diary. I'd give myself complete permission to write the truth about a fear or hang-up or part of myself I didn't like without judgment or self-censorship. If I could freely admit everything to myself with no fear of censure or guilt, at least I'd know what I was really dealing with.

Any journey into shadow work is not about getting lost in the darkness but about illuminating it, accepting it, and, in the process, transforming what you find into a source of strength and self-awareness.

It was by engaging in this process that I realized my so-called dream job doing marketing for a tech company was someone else's vision and not my own. Anxious to find my place in the world, I had gone so far into my adult, responsible self that I had forgotten about the child inside me.

You have probably heard of the term "the inner child." You may even have a clear vision of your own: the inner child is the "little you" you may have forgotten about or who was neglected by the conditions of your upbringing, but who still calls out, from deep inside you, to play, create, self-soothe, or cry. It was Jung who came up with the concept of the inner child, and it was Jung who argued that we all needed to meet, listen to, and heal that part of us before we can truly become who we were meant to be. He wrote, "In every adult there lurks a child—an eternal child, something that is always becoming, is never completed, and calls for unceasing care, attention, and education. That is the part of the personality which wants to develop and become whole."[1] If you close your eyes and ask, your inner child will reveal itself to you, in all its emotional distress and mischievousness and capacity for boundless joy.

Much of doing shadow work, I discovered, was welcoming my wounded inner child into my waking adult life: identifying her needs and finding opportunities to allow her to express herself, unencumbered by conventional notions of how I was supposed to be. So, as I continued on the path of shadow work, I naturally asked myself, "What are my abandoned passions?"

I quickly flashed onto how I had all but abandoned playing the flute. It had once been such a sustaining activity for me, and I dropped it in search of a more "responsible adult life." I kept going. One realization led to another, and another, and with each one came another liberation. It turns out that shadow work is a lifelong process, and that's just fine. I took pieces of myself on, one at a time, because none of us can know the truth all at once, we can just meet it as it comes, bathing each instance of pain in acceptance until eventually neither the light nor the darkness overpowers the other. In the clarity gained from a true, full perspective, you see how much space there is between you and your shackles. That's real freedom.

In 2021, after a period rich with introspection and discovery, I asked myself, "Why doesn't everyone know about shadow work? Why don't more people talk about it?" With each revelation of another hidden part of myself, each moment of recognition, through journaling and mirror work, and those 4 a.m. mornings of searching, bit by bit I healed my inner child. Not only healed her—I gave her some powerful tools. I reincorporated play into my life. I began going on hikes, looking for fossils like I used to when I went camping as a kid. I picked up the flute again and explored sound healing, which allowed me to soothe my inner world during moments of anxiety. I remembered how to be curious and expressive. I decided to open up and release whenever I felt like I was contracting and holding in. What came out of all that was healing. In moments when I could have broken down, I was able to create a new path for me to break *through*.

Meeting, understanding, and accepting my own shadow sparked a profound transformation in me that only continues to accelerate the more I feed it. I realized next that I needed to share the process I had put together for myself with the rest of the world.

I got the idea to create a simple workbook, with clear prompts and cues, in plain language, to guide people through doing their own shadow work. If I could do it, I figured, anyone could. They just needed tools they could understand and an easy way to get started. I felt inspired to support Jung's late-in-life mission to bring his teachings to a wider audience, too. Jung's publisher had been frustrated that while his mentor Sigmund Freud's work was well-known, Jung's contribution remained inaccessible. It took

Jung having an important dream one night to get him to move on it, though. In that dream, he saw himself addressing an audience who truly understood him. Finally, right before his death, he wrote a book with a lay public in mind. It's called *Man and His Symbols*,[2] and I highly recommend it.

Jung's desire to reach a broader audience beyond academia reaffirmed my commitment to this project. It felt like a continuation of Jung's mission, a way to honor his legacy by helping others embark on their own journeys of self-discovery and transformation. I do not take a strict or orthodox approach to Jung. I am not a credentialed Jung scholar or a trained Jungian analyst, but I didn't have to be for his work to empower and inspire me, and I wanted that for other people too. I didn't see what I was doing as a substitute for therapy, either. Despite my initial bad experience, I revere the work of counselors and shrinks. But I also know that therapy remains out of reach for a lot of people and that we all can do much to bring healing to ourselves.

The idea ignited a fire within me. I felt as if I was tapping directly into a divine source, in harmony with every part of myself. This wasn't just a project; it was a calling. I felt a deep responsibility to bring this work into the light in the best way I could, to help others navigate the complexities of their inner worlds with kindness. Engaging in intentional self-reflection at the peak of a trigger can halt the destruction before it takes over our bodies and minds. I saw this as a tool for awareness before turmoil and an approachable start to a life-transforming healing journey. It could ease the suffering of millions, a little or a lot, if I got it right.

Creating that journal became my lifeline. It drew me back into wholeness, allowed me to reclaim my own authenticity and put myself back together.

I never anticipated it would have such a profound impact. Since I published *The Shadow Work Journal* at the end of 2021, its reach has been extraordinary. In 2023 alone, over one million copies were purchased, and it was recognized as an Amazon number-one bestseller four times. *The Shadow Work Journal* has not only received over forty thousand five-star reviews from readers around the world, it has garnered immense support from social media and even caught the attention of legacy media, featured on *Good Morning America* and in the pages of the *Atlantic* and the *New York Times*. Therapists started to contact me to say they were using *The Shadow Work Journal* as a tool with their patients. And journalers created a supportive community, via social media, sharing their experiences with the world.

The Shadow Work Journal's widespread acclaim speaks volumes about its efficacy and resonance with those seeking deeper self-understanding. It illuminated how universal human suffering and pain are and how everyone has a soul that wanders the desert of existence, searching for a divine source to keep going. We all need softness, depth, and meaning to navigate the harsh, boxed-in, artificial world we live in. No matter how deeply we may find ourselves in despair, there is always a path that leads back to our essence, to that inner bright flame that can guide us through our darkest moments.

We haven't been alone. The practice of delving deep into the self, of exploring the shadows and light within, is experiencing a global renaissance. People from all walks of life are awakening to the importance of self-exploration, recognizing that true understanding and growth are in our own hands and souls. *The Shadow Work Journal* has proven itself to be a valuable tool, but there was context and insight I gathered during the process of writing it that necessarily got left on the cutting-room floor. *The Journal* is a starting point for something much bigger. A baby step in my journey, and maybe in yours.

With this book, I wanted to write something more expansive than a workbook—more like a primer or a comprehensive guide to how shadow work unfolds on a grander scale, and what we can all do to better meet and mesh with our shadows. Here there is more context and material for continued reflection, wise perspective from experienced experts, tips and stories from people who took the plunge into shadow work for the first time, and expanded techniques and resources to facilitate greater self-healing. *The Shadow Work Journal*, with billions of social media engagements and thousands of testimonials, is part of a long chain of human self-inquiry. The book you're now holding, *The Book of Shadow Work*, shines a brighter light on that chain and looks back to explain how the shadow, and shadow work too, has been present in religion, literature, and ritual throughout time and history. I also wanted readers to benefit from understanding more of the *why* behind the global reach of shadow work, from the many conversations I've had with therapists, thinkers, teachers, and healers since the publication of *The Shadow Work Journal*, to capture how shadow work, as a set of diverse practices, continues to evolve.

The Book of Shadow Work joins all our hands in collective awareness and the search for truth. This is an exploratory book, and I am the navigator. I know you will find gems along the way just by opening your heart and allowing the words to press against your soul wherever it feels tender. Whenever it pangs with resonance, that is a spark of light, and more will follow. In that sense, this book is not just an essential companion to *The Shadow Work Journal*, but a bigger, more fulsome road map for anyone seeking to deepen their self-awareness and heal their inner wounds. It offers insights and guidance toward a deeper understanding of yourself and the world around you and includes inspiring stories and tips from the community that has sprung up around my company, Zenfulnote, illustrating the expanding power of shadow work to radically improve daily life, relationships, trauma, the stress of making your way in the world, and society at large. These bits of good news are like finding golden apples on the darkest parts of the yellow brick road, and this book is filled with them.

My strongest wish is that the experience of reading this book will be transformational for anyone who takes it seriously. My intention is clear: by the time you reach the end, you will not only have a richer understanding of what shadow work is, you will be empowered to play and dance with your inner self, and you will meet your unconscious and experience moments of transformation where once you simply might have felt out of control. Profound revelations, renewed emotional stability, and resilience can be yours if you let them come.

There is another payoff with shadow work that I hope this book will help you put into motion. When you begin to live authentically, to speak and act in harmony with your true self, your life inevitably shifts. When you begin to show up as all of yourself—loudly and proudly, or even softly and subtly—the people who are meant for you will start to take notice. They won't just hear you; they'll connect with the essence of who you are. They'll find joy in your presence and value in your words. If you're feeling afraid about showing up in the world as the real you, remember that this fear is not yours to bear alone.

Remember also that you are infinitely more than the sum of any imposed identities. Your inherent worth lies in your authenticity, in being seen and loved for who you truly are. Your unapologetic self is not just a right; it's a beacon for others, modeling for them how to find their own truth.

How do you start? Turn the page with an open heart and open mind, and consider gently peeling away the layers that aren't truly you. The universe has got your back. I've got your back too.

ONE

WHAT IS SHADOW WORK? HOW DO YOU START?

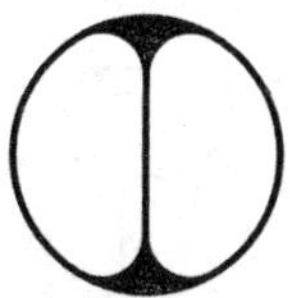

Everyone carries a shadow, and the less it is embodied in the individual's conscious life, the blacker and denser it is.

If an inferiority is conscious, one always has a chance to correct it. . . .

But if it is repressed and isolated from consciousness, it never gets corrected.

—C. G. JUNG, *PSYCHOLOGY AND WESTERN RELIGION*[I]

Sometimes the things that break your heart end up fixing your vision.

—MUSICAL ARTIST UNKONFINED

The shadow sounds scary, doesn't it? Dark, ominous, formless, foreboding, morally shady, elusive, creepy, even evil. When we talk about the shadow as Jung defined it—the part of our unconscious mind that contains what we reject and hide from—the very thought of its existence can put us on edge, like we're not really our own masters. Like we're carrying around this bag of toxic garbage, and it's weighing us down. But according to Jung, the shadow will always be with us, and it serves a clear purpose. It's not trash; it's compost.

I always knew, even before I read Jung, that childhood experiences laid the foundation of our emotional frameworks. Traumas leave imprints. They shape our reactions, our fears, and our joys, and then as we grow, they get buried under the façade of responsible adulthood. When these old wounds are triggered, the reaction is often disproportionate to the present situation, leaving us confused and overwhelmed. It's a journey to unpack these layers, to understand that our present self is in constant dialogue with the shadows of the past, and the shadow of the present too. Acknowledging this is not a sign of weakness; it's an act of bravery, a step toward healing not just the present, but also the past that silently guides us.

Can you imagine yourself as a small child, born helpless into a family with its own dynamics and value systems? You knew, even in infancy, that you needed to adjust to the powers that be to survive. As you started to understand how some behaviors or moods got rewards or punishments, you shape-shifted to your best advantage, structured your inner world, and showed up accordingly. Was your nature, or your behavior, considered too loud? Too needy? Too competitive? Too sad? Too hungry? Too angry? Too sensitive? Too shy? You learned that Mom and/or Dad didn't approve. Society didn't approve. Red alert. Start camouflaging yourself, even from yourself.

It is the self-preserving, self-protective part of us that pushes away what is deemed unlovable, unacceptable, and dangerous by our families and the larger world. As we grow up, that lifesaving reflex develops into a crucial skill for getting by. What is successful moves into the limelight. Everything left over that doesn't fit, that feels shameful or enraging or destabilizing, or even too brilliant and visionary, is relegated to the shadow.

It is the self-preserving, self-protective part of us that pushes away what is deemed unlovable, unacceptable, and dangerous by our families and the larger world.

The shadow may primarily dwell outside daily consciousness, but it never stays fully hidden. It impacts our beliefs at the edges of our awareness, erupting into waking life at the most inconvenient times. It emerges, sometimes with overwhelming force, when we're shaken, triggered, heartbroken, scared, angry, jealous, or in crisis. It rules compulsions and addictions, irrational-seeming fears and unhealed traumas. Sometimes the shadow takes control when things are going so well that we can't believe it. It comes along to help us sabotage ourselves to maintain safe equilibrium, no matter how dull and empty it's become.

Jung believed this dynamic was common to all humans since the birth of our species. So, if we have all always had a shadow, then how can having a shadow be wrong? Jung refused to moralize the question. To the contrary, he felt that the modern world and Western religions' tendency to insist on rigid dichotomies of good and evil gave the shadow even greater destructive potential by pushing it further out of conscious reach. The harder we try to deny our shadows, the more we villainize, other them, and proclaim ourselves as better than all that, the stronger they become.

"I never had a safe space to express my emotions when I was a little girl," says Violet, thirty, a content creator living in Seattle. "I got yelled at for having the smallest issue. I couldn't cry, I couldn't talk, I couldn't do anything." Having to live in silence when you are a child, at your most naturally spontaneous, exuberant, and curious, is understandably enraging. Because of her family's rules, the intense anger at being so heavily censored that Violet carried around most of her life got pushed into her shadow. There it simmered just outside her consciousness, often bubbling up inappropriately, even more so as she became an adult. "It was easier to just shoo my kids away and avoid my anger, so I didn't get overwhelmed," she says of the short fuse that was naturally set off all too often as a single working mother.

Avoiding the anger deprived Violet's children of real intimacy with the most important person in their lives and deepened her sense of guilt over behavior whose origins she didn't fully understand. It became a vicious cycle until she had had enough. Violet has decades of experience with mental health professionals, including a productive history with cognitive behavioral therapy and dialectical behavioral therapy. Those approaches have immense and clinically proven value, but they primarily focus on the adaptive structure of the conscious mind and the ego—the parts of ourselves closest in reach, and that we can most easily adjust and change by reframing our thought patterns and behavior. These are crucial sites for clarity and healing, and they play a role in shadow work too, when we put ourselves back together and integrate after having taken ourselves apart. But those therapies alone weren't sufficient to address what Violet felt calling her, from somewhere deeper down below. She knew she needed to look beyond her behavior and her adult coping mechanisms. She needed to untangle what had been strangling her inner child. That's when she started doing shadow work and realizing just how much her upbringing held her back in her work, in her relationships, and with her kids.

Jung defined the shadow not just as the seat of so-called negative emotions and complexes, but as a rich and meaningful part of the greater self, crying out to be consciously acknowledged and integrated into a healthier, more vibrant whole. Integrating that through shadow work can be an intimidating idea, but it is not a penance. It is a hunt for treasure. And besides, life demands pushing our limits to thrive. For humans, that means facing our greatest darkness.

In the early 1990s, scientists conducted an experiment in the Arizona desert called Biosphere 2. The objective of the project was to re-create Earth's ecosystems inside a sealed structure so that scientists could explore the potential of supporting life on another planet. The total ground area spanned over three acres, containing various microcosms of the planet.

The scientists lived inside this closed ecological system for two years, and at one point in their experiment, they were puzzled by a discovery: the trees inside Biosphere 2 grew faster than their counterparts in the wild, yet they fell before reaching maturity. How could the trees grow so rapidly yet die unexpectedly? The scientists studied this phenomenon further, and they reached a surprising conclusion: trees need wind to grow to their full capacity. Since the Biosphere 2 was contained and protected, it lacked the cosseting and challenge that would be present in the real world. The stress of wind pushing against a tree's trunks causes its root system to grow deep and strong and its trunk to become sturdier. Stress from the elements is essential for their growth and survival.

Those of us desperate to shield the wind of life, the radical friction of being, and the adversity that comes with it are Biosphere 2 trees. Just as they needed the wind to grow strong and resilient, we, too, require challenges and changes to develop psychological and emotional robustness and come closer to fulfilling our limitless potential.

Like trees trying to escape the wind, humankind has devised numerous ways to avoid the discomforts of life's stressors, wildly repressing our emotions, turning to substances, compulsive scrolling, or obsessively positive thinking to numb our experiences and mask our truths.

Conversely, sometimes we might overidentify with our wounds. As we better understand trauma and suffering today, some of us might be tempted to see them as inescapable, crippling conditions and assume their trauma as their whole identity, a painful diagnosis or episode as the end of the story rather than a new chapter with its own potential for incredible evolution. This misconception can make us retreat into our shells, nursing what hurts us in isolation, believing that to show our scars is to show weakness. To be weak is to be needy, to court exploitation and rejection. Most of us have heard of post-traumatic stress disorder. How many of us have heard of its very real counterpart, post-traumatic stress growth?

Escapism provides a temporary relief, but suffering is an essential component of the human condition. Viewing the shadow as part of a healthy ecosystem, like Jung did, takes us out of victimhood. We are the ones who created our shadows, and we, too, possess the ability to bring them back into the light, back into our own sight, to confront our deepest fears, question the narratives we've constructed about our identity and worth, and reforge our relationship with ourselves and the world around us. It's not the presence of pain that defines us, but how we face it and what we do with it that counts. Shadow work is often an exercise in understanding how that which doesn't kill us makes us stronger.

Escapism provides a temporary relief, but suffering is an essential component of the human condition.

It takes courage to uncover and sit with what your conscious mind and ego don't approve of and give that dark, rejected part of you the space to speak and breathe and shine.

Unlike many other self-help practices, shadow work is more about letting go than adding on. It's about releasing the false identities and the roles you've played for the approval of others, unraveling the masks, and looking behind the personae that have been hiding your true self. While the ego may uphold the existing order, it's the discomfort of the shadow that acts as a force for change and transformation. The ego creates, and the shadow destroys. To learn who you are, you have to unlearn who you were told to be.

Unlike many other self-help practices, shadow work is more about letting go than adding on.

Many psychological practices are designed to fix perceived weaknesses, subtly imposing a stigma on "problem" parts. Sometimes this simply aligns with the ego's goals: constant happiness, maintaining appearances, boosting productivity, feeling accomplished, and exerting control. But the shadow needs a voice and space to be, in all its messiness. Shadow work does not cater to ego desires and needs. When doing shadow work, things can get a little uncomfortable, especially at first. As you go along and start to experience the benefits of greater authenticity and healthier and deeper connections, it becomes easier to love the fertile ground of your soul, even if it's a little dirty, because that's where you uncover hidden gold.

Shadow work teases out your potentially destructive patterns and asks you to explore them with curiosity rather than fear, eventually embracing them as valuable parts of you. It is a deeply personal, therapeutic journey where you create a safe container, either alone or with guidance, to observe and dialogue with yourself, and ultimately integrate what you discover into a richer, healthier wholeness. The goal of this work isn't to wallow in pain but to know what causes it, in the light of self-acceptance and understanding. Nor is it to banish the darkness, but to welcome it, understanding that what you once sought to render invisible is as important a part of you as the palatable mask you've created to get by.

Given the amazing buffet of mental health treatment options out there today, it's worth asking how to know if you need shadow work rather than some other kind of therapy or self-help practice. My feeling is that, because the shadow is always part of us, there's never anything to be lost by going deep, and doing so often.

Benjamin Bernstein, a shaman, astrologer, and author of *Instant Divine Assistance*,[2] sees the shadow work prescription in even more general terms: "If everything's bright and shiny and happy, then you're probably good for now," he says. "But if something is disturbing you emotionally, even physically, on any level, if there's anything that doesn't feel absolutely wonderful, then there's some shadow work there to be done." In his Asheville, North Carolina–based practice, Bernstein sees individual shadow work as an essential part of the spiritual evolution of the planet.

You can be sure your shadow is speaking when you find yourself irked by qualities in others that mirror your own suppressed traits. When you experience unexplained jealousy or envy of someone else's success or happiness, it can offer a reflection of your unfulfilled desires or unrecognized potential that you have pushed into your shadow. When your inner critic is far harsher than any overt external judgment, look to your shadow. Or if you're plagued by persistent dreams, or you keep coming back to the same enraging, or terrifying, or deeply sad memories, with no diminution of the emotional charge around them; or you're simply feeling stuck in a compulsive pattern of behavior you can't seem to shake, no matter how marvelous outside reality seems to be. The shadow finds painful ironies in daily life: maybe you experience profound disconnection or loneliness when you're surrounded by your friends.

There are many kinds of shadow work you can do and many resources out there to help you do it. One reason I decided to write this book was to better broadcast those resources in their rich diversity. But first, some important caveats to heed. If you have ever been diagnosed with schizophrenia or have had manic episodes that involve hallucinations or delusions, do not attempt this work without the accompaniment of a trusted mental health professional, as shadow work requires voyaging into the unconscious, which is boundless and unpredictable. A history of bipolar disorder or any experience of psychosis should put guided psilocybin trips, a kind of shadow work with rich potential, off-limits. If you have started to do shadow work by journaling, dream analysis, guided meditation, or any of the many other techniques we'll touch on and you have had thoughts of suicide, stop and seek outside help. Doing shadow work can shake most people's emotional foundations, but it should never put you in danger.

I created *The Shadow Work Journal*, but I don't see the processes and exercises there as the only way to get to the shadow. I didn't call it shadow work when I was a little girl going to church in my hometown of Houston, even if that practice from my childhood bore a striking resemblance to it. Each time I prepared for confession at my local chapel, I used a small booklet to jot down everything that weighed on my heart—essentially an inventory of my youthful transgressions. This ritual wasn't labeled as such, but in essence it was an early foray into acknowledging and confronting my own darkness.

In the days leading up to confession, I would reflect on the past few months, noting any instances when I acted out of anger, judged someone too harshly, or allowed selfish thoughts to guide me. As a young girl, my "sins" were often trivial. One was gluttony—sneaking extra candy from the pantry and hoarding it. Another was responding to my brother with unnecessary sharpness. Despite the seemingly low stakes of these acts, cataloging them stirred a familiar nervousness within me, a sensation so many people encounter when facing their shadow selves. For little Keila, the act of confession itself, especially when it was met with compassion by our parish priest rather than condemnation, was liberating. It was as if by naming these hidden parts of myself—those driven by basic, almost primal desires for pleasure or rebellion—I was freed from their weight.

In small and big ways, shadow work is happening all around you, day and night. It's anywhere that people find a way into contact with their unconscious and face what they find with forgiveness and compassion, holding space for their darkness as well as their light.

Many people start shadow work in a therapist's office, doing dream analysis, hypnosis, breath work, or even neurologically oriented trauma-repair techniques like EMDR or Brainspotting. Shadow work happens in nonclinical settings, too. Julianna Rees is a drama coach and teacher who codesigned the curriculum of the Conservatory Theater Ensemble of Tamalpais High School in Mill Valley, California. Since the implementation of Konstantin Stanislavski's technique—what most people now call "Method acting"—to mid-twentieth-century theater, Rees explains that people studying drama have learned to get in touch with their painful emotions and memories to bring the fullest life to their characters. The purpose for actors isn't to relive their own trauma every time they go to work, especially the student actors who have been Rees's main focus. That would be dangerous for their mental health. But in learning how to express emotion, regularly, on time, on cue, and in a truthful way, young actors must pass through uncomfortable territory that usually includes their own experiences. Rees has created exercises to help them explore these emotions safely so they can reimagine them without having to reexperience them every time they're called. In the process, there is much growth.

Many people I've spoken to for this book told me that they felt called to go inward because they were suffering. Some of them had truly hit rock bottom, experiencing what Jung called the dark night of the soul—that moment when everything has fallen apart and your only way to take a step forward through tragedy is to reclaim and radically change your relationship to yourself. Jung went through his own dark night of the soul as a young psychoanalyst, after a painful separation from his mentor, Sigmund Freud. The self-guided work that Jung undertook to heal from that devastating experience, including a profound confrontation with his shadow, became the basis of his most radical breakthroughs.

Sometimes the situation is so dire that heeding the inner call to evolution is the only thing you have any control over. Johnny, forty, an Army veteran and mechanic from Brazoria, Texas, had just walked out of a well-paying job and a toxic marriage and was facing losing his home and shared custody of his two kids, when he really dove into himself.

His first experience of shadow work was going through the "ruthless moral inventory" of the fourth step in Alcoholics Anonymous. This is the infamous "scary step" when addicts are encouraged to identify negative emotions and patterns that have contributed to their addictions—material that lives in their shadows—including harmful behavior toward and betrayals of the people they love the most. They face this personal material in supportive community with other addicts, in a context of both ruthless honesty and radical self-forgiveness—key to being able to revisit and integrate shadow triggers and traumas without causing more of them in the present through shame and self-recrimination. Johnny attended daily AA meetings for months, gradually tapering down to once a week, as he developed additional shadow work practices of daily journaling and meditation. As he has faced his dark side and created a loving space inside himself by accepting it, his temper and emotional reactivity have faded. He has become a better listener and father. "I'm falling back in love with life," he says.

Nicole DeMartine, PhD, a healing practitioner based in Little Ferry, New Jersey, took her first step into shadow work over two decades ago, after a series of revelations about her family caused her to investigate her roots. What she found pointed the way to exploring deeper and more profound ways to approach her own pain. "When I was nine, I realized I had a different father than I had been told, and finally met him when I was sixteen," she recalls. "His grandmother was a full-blooded Choctaw Indian from Oklahoma, and so I started learning about Native American history and spirituality." In this investigation, DeMartine caught a glimpse of who she could be away from her mother's heavy influence and discovered practices connected to her real ancestry that led her to emotional freedom. She started going to shamanic workshops and participating in plant medicine ceremonies, indigenous shadow-healing paths we will look at more closely in the next chapter. "That was really what started me on my shadow work journey."

What makes something shadow work? First, it is in the willingness to go deeper than cognitive and behavioral analysis to reach into your unconscious mind. Where Freud saw the unconscious mostly as a place of neurosis and dysfunction, Jung was more curious and forgiving, more accepting and adventurous, because he found human brilliance there too, even in a space where contemporary morals and good behavior have no primacy. The other crucial shadow work difference is in the profound acceptance of that dark material as part of you, rather than judging it or trying to work around it as if it could simply be forgotten or retrained or "overcome."

Different people resonate with different shadow work techniques. Josh, thirty-three, an English teacher living in Batumi, Georgia, took his first step into shadow work creatively, alone, by composing affirmations after walking away from a high-control religion. Not all affirmation practices are the same. Josh's practice plunged into his lived unhappiness and what had motivated his life choices, to understand what was missing from the inside out. "I had such low self-esteem and just felt ugly all around," he says. "I had one notebook where I'd write the negative things that were on my mind, and then I'd turn them around into positive things." Only after he really understood the darkness—how guilty his religion made him feel about the simplest things; how shut down he had become trying to conform—could he write a new story for himself that had any hope of feeling true.

Through the experience, which he bolstered with a regular journaling practice, Josh rediscovered his voice. "Engaging with my shadow was so uncomfortable at first, because I reunited with a part of myself I had lost, and that I missed so much. I was an emotional, feeling person once. My wife told me that I had been almost silent for the last ten years, where once I was outgoing and confident and fun. I am meeting that person again, learning to let go, enjoy life, and not tie myself to guilt or perfection."

When I took my own first plunge into shadow work as a grown-up, I experimented with practices that were totally new to me, like sitting in front of my reflection in the mirror and engaging in honest dialogue with myself. It wasn't about assessing whether I looked good, or *was* good, it was about seeing beyond the surface and letting it exist. I poured out my heart and my disappointments and just listened to myself. In my own eyes, I found a realm of truth where doubts and sadness lived unmasked, and as I was able to see it in myself, in real time, I had compassion for myself. Those mirror sessions, conversations with the deepest parts of me, pulled me into moments of intense honesty and vulnerability and showed me that I could trust myself with myself, because my own eyes didn't lie.

Importantly, like Josh, I would finish emotional episodes of self-confrontation with positive words of affirmation. It was like weaving threads of light into my energy. Each positive statement was a custom-made counter to the doubts and fears that I now more fully understood and accepted, a reminder of my strength and worth and capacity to grow. This part of my emerging practice helped reclaim my self-worth and resilience, and it brought more levity and joy into the shadow work process. It also showed me that I wasn't just the voice in my head, I was also the listener, the observer of that voice, and the wise and comforting woman who spoke back. Shadow work can be intense and challenging, stripping away masks and illusions. But it's incomplete and harder to come back to if it doesn't also include positive reinforcement. We'll return to a deeper discussion of the integrative aspect of shadow work in Chapter Eight.

Given the potential for discomfort and intense emotional release in doing shadow work, how much is too much? "Some people might want to do something every day," says DeMartine, who incorporates shadow work into her practice with her clients, across modalities that include Kundalini yoga, Reiki, and quantum healing, which maps emotional triggers onto different points on the body. "Some people do it once a week. For people with ADHD, like me, I find it hard to get into any kind of routine. I think it's really useful to start with journaling, because it's such a good way to talk to your own unconscious mind. But at the end of the day, find what works best for you and keep at it."

If you've decided to seek out a mental health practitioner to do shadow work, use your best judgment. It's important that anyone who endeavors to guide people through such deep and often triggering territory continues to work on their own shadows too. Shadow work is powerful and vulnerable, for both healer and patient. "I had a pretty rough childhood," says DeMartine. "My mom struggled with addiction and her mental health, and I watched her suffer a lot growing up. It's probably how a lot of people in the healing industry (find their paths), because we come from trauma, right?"

Listen to yourself if you feel that sharing intimately with a counselor is turning into exploitation or a power trip. Anne Whitaker, seventy-seven, is an astrologer in Glasgow, Scotland, who understands the temptation to seem all-knowing, which encourages unhealthy dependency in clients. An eagerness to show off skills can bluster through a situation that calls for far greater delicacy and care. As an astrologer with a background in teaching, social work, and psychology, as she reads clients' charts, she goes the softest when she sees potential signatures of trauma. She recalls one client, a much older woman, whose chart showed indications of possible sexual abuse at age seven. "If, just to show how clever I was, I just came out and said to her, 'I think you were sexually abused when you were seven,' that would have been me abusing her all over again," she explains. "But I had already worked a lot with my own capacity to be abusive. If you can own it in yourself, you can exercise moral control over it, see it coming up, and decide how to channel it in a constructive direction."

Insist on rules and boundaries for consent and know that sometimes going slowly is the only way to build trust with a practitioner.

This is not the same thing as normal resistance. Especially at the beginning of the process, filling out those first pages in your journal or sharing a difficult dream for the first time, it is normal to get squeamish exploring your dark side, either alone or with a guide. This can mean looking at your journal with side-eye, or skipping out on therapy appointments, or deciding maybe there isn't time for meditation today. That happens to everyone, and it's not the same thing as feeling ill inside when you are asked to go beyond your healthy limits.

Build in some buffers. Make sure that whichever method you choose, you include conscious self-respect and downtime. Honor yourself when emotional processing makes you tired, as any intense experience can. Schedule a few hours, or a day, if you have it, to drift and recover after peeling back another layer of yourself. Engage purposefully in self-care. Drink more water. Do what you can to get more sleep. (Chances are, your dreams will be especially memorable now anyway.) Call on support networks of trusted family, friends, and community to feel their warmth and love as you journey forth, even if you decide not to share with them everything you're doing. I've found that doing shadow work increases my capacity to love and connect. You may find yourself basking in levels of love you never knew were there before.

Treating your shadow with reverence and respect, not fleeing from it compulsively or numbing it away with distraction, will pay you back ten thousand times over. You can not only achieve a greater sense of wholeness and self-acceptance but unlock pathways to healing and self-discovery that were previously obscured by fears or prejudices. Hidden talents come to life. Sustaining passions emerge. Joy deepens. Compassion grows. Intimacy and connection to others too. Purpose and resiliency are claimed. Manifesting happens more effortlessly. We are simply more in the zone.

Ultimately, shadow work, at whatever frequency you choose, is a lifelong path, one that brings greater rewards the more you do it. No matter where you are in the process, know that in jumping into the ocean of your unconscious, you will resurface as a changed person.

Isn't that the point? Humans are not designed to remain static, replaying old narratives day after day, reenacting them in every aspect of existence. Like strong trees, we are meant to grow beyond them. Being human means we are never at a final state. We are perpetually in the process of becoming, unfolding, learning, growing, and transforming. There's no such thing as a "fully healed" version of you, where finally all the drama is over. Healing is always in process, as is simply being. Shadow work facilitates the shedding of our old layers, allowing the embrace of new beginnings. What new version of yourself will you step into? What more genuine expressions of *you* will you start to embody?

TWO

A FIELD GUIDE TO THE EMOTIONS

We should not pretend to understand the world only by the intellect; we apprehend it just as much by feeling. Therefore, the judgment of the intellect is at best only a half-truth and must, if it is honest, also admit its inadequacy.

—C.G. JUNG, *PSYCHOLOGICAL TYPES*[1]

In doing shadow work, you're going to feel, and you're going to feel deeply.

As much as shadow work involves using memory to root out events and associations you pushed into your unconscious mind in the past, it is not done from an entirely cerebral place. Shadow work is certainly partly a thought process—especially when you first begin, you will make new connections between experiences past and present. You might find yourself better remembering your dreams. You may uncover long-forgotten memories or whole parts of your past. All this is crucial to rewriting your personal history with a more compassionate and fuller understanding of who you were when you were little and who you are today.

But shadow work is also an emotional process, and in many ways emotions have a more fluid connection to the unconscious, where the shadow lies. To me this is shadow work's greatest gift. Get into the habit of allowing yourself to fully feel what comes up and respect its truth, not only when you're doing shadow work, but also in daily life. What I discovered after I had been engaged in shadow work for a while was that staying laser-focused on how I felt—in my heart and crucially, in my body—and sitting with it without judgment became a cosmic superpower. Clearing out a more respectful emotional space for myself gave me honesty. It gave me the strength and resilience to face new challenges with less stress. It gave me easier access to my creativity, inspiration, and deeper parts of my unconscious mind. It pointed the way to decision-making from a more authentic place, because rather than impose an outcome I thought would be good for me, I started searching out how I felt first and giving that primary importance.

There's quiet power in following your path, even when you walk it alone. Honor your journey. My realization that I was in the wrong career wouldn't have happened if I hadn't been able to lean into my feelings through shadow work and trust them to guide me. If I had let my brain and ambitions and what my family wanted for me take over, I'd still be miserable, in a confining job that didn't reflect my real gifts and dreams.

There's quiet power in following your path, even when you walk it alone. Honor your journey.

It's worth it for everyone to learn how to do this, and not just to make better decisions or have more abundant outcomes. Our emotions are much more profound than that. Feeling is the greatest gift of our human and animal nature. It's not simply a function of us, part of our mammalian social survival skill set, to be mastered and controlled. Feelings deserve to remain a little wild, even when they are not sweet. They are the source of our beauty and mystery, a required part of being truly alive. Without feeling, sometimes strong feeling, there can be no art, no spirituality, no transcendence; it is the lifeblood that animates our deepest expressions and connects us to the sublime.

Allowing yourself to acknowledge and express your feelings, past and present, without judgment, centers you in yourself. It is a profound act of self-honoring. It makes you the subject of your story, not an inconvenience to be overcome. It gives you an express route to your own truth and healing. The intellect can lie. It loves to gaslight. Feelings cannot. They're as important as reading the newspaper to understanding how you're really living. But unlike the newspaper in static black and white, they can be elusive, slippery, and require a different kind of perception. They're meant to be experienced in real time, with no CliffsNotes or shortcuts. It's only when you let them be that you get the benefit of their wisdom.

Consider this: we are born sobbing. Since birth, our cries showed not that we were weak but that we were alive. As we evolved and grew, those cries become rarer and more seldomly expressed. If we're lucky, we learned to release emotion in "acceptable" or romanticized ways, like singing or painting or dancing. Then those emotions, rather than coming out as sour droplets, were built into something intentional through instruments of our bodies. Vocal cords transform raw feeling into melodies and harmonies, hands paint pictures and form sculpture.

Art and music and dance bring diverse groups of people together, in one room, or on one lawn, in shared trance. The next time you go to an art gallery or watch a recorded live music set on YouTube, watch the crowd: You'll see a business guy with a fanny pack doing the doggy paddle, a kid with oversize sunglasses, a mermaid-haired girl in her flow state. This kind of emotional expression is universal, uniting people across great divides.

I like to think of emotion as energy in motion. I promise you it is better to give this energy room to dance unfettered, to change and evolve—which it almost always does—rather than try to clamp it down and tame it into silence. When feelings are given their proper place, at the center of your lived experience, and acknowledged in real time, even if you can't always fully express them in that moment, it becomes a lot easier to handle the challenging ones, like anger, panic, sadness, and fear. It can take practice to get there and can require some originality in method, but once you do, you never turn back. You don't want to.

For many people, being asked to dive into their emotions is a terrifying idea. For those who have lived more comfortably in their heads most of their life, it is almost a foreign concept. For those who have done so as if with no choice, like with neurodivergence, they might have a harder time clearly accessing, expressing, and managing their emotions, so they need to find new pathways that will be theirs alone. Because of how it invites you to experience and claim your feelings in their uniqueness and express them using your own creativity, shadow work is an empowering space to experiment with that.

A word of firm advice: when you're doing shadow work, don't barge into your most disturbing memories and vulnerable feeling states with guns blazing. It takes time for the inner self to trust. Don't try to dive straight to the bottom of the well right away. Accessing troubling feelings and memories slowly, delicately, and with great care, so as not to flood yourself with sensation, is wisdom learned from therapists like Peter Levine, PhD, author of, most recently, *An Autobiography of Trauma: A Healing Journey.*[2] Levine is the founder of Somatic Experiencing therapy, a pioneer of body-centered healing. His concern holds for everyone, no matter how resilient or experienced they are when they come to shadow work, whether they have received a diagnosis of trauma or PTSD or not. A light touch is the rule. Taking breaks is the rule. Cultivating empathy for yourself is the rule.

A word of firm advice: when you're doing shadow work, don't barge into your most disturbing memories and vulnerable feeling states with guns blazing.

For people who have experienced trauma, which includes many of us, their emotional compass may be in a state of shutdown. It could be stuck in the quadrant of panic or rage or terror or sadness, which can be unbearably stressful to live through every day. For people who have suffered serious trauma or experience heavier forms of PTSD, and so need to approach traumatic memories carefully and with containment, it can be helpful to do shadow work with a trained trauma therapist.

For some people, emotions that were unbearable for them to feel, or dangerous for them to express, might have been muted from their conscious awareness by dissociation, or by deadening and disconnecting from the feeling state and essentially going numb. "When there's a lot of stress, what happens is we develop a phobic avoidance to sensation or experience," says therapist Esther Goldstein, LCSW.[3] This includes bright, loud emotions in all their colors, even the joyful ones. Dissociation can be a transitory response to stress, rather than lived as a steady state, but the more time you spend in it, the more you miss out on a full life.

So many people I have spoken to for this book were discouraged from showing their feelings as children. Violet, whom you met in the last chapter, is a classic example of someone whose emotional expression was overwhelming to her mother, who was already in her own state of meltdown. Violet learned to turn the volume down on everything, at great cost to her well-being. In doing shadow work, she has gained more access to her full emotional spectrum and has more useful conscious experience watching it work. This makes even the taboo emotions like anger and sadness easier for her to handle because she has developed skills. One of them is a greater capacity for self-love.

For Lawrence, thirty-one, who lives in New York City, it was his mother who took up all the emotional space when he was growing up, leaving little room for anyone else. "My mom was, and still is, the heartbeat of the family," he says. "If she's doing well, we're all doing well. If she's not doing well, we're going to hear about it, and we're not going to be doing well either. On family vacations, when my parents would fight, my brother would chime in with something stupid, and then they'd just yell at him. So, I became the fixer and problem solver in the family." This meant Lawrence had no incentive to recognize and immerse himself in his emotions, because he feared they would have just added more fuel to the existing chaos. Left unheeded, his more painful emotions reemerged as anxious vigilance. He was overly tuned in to the turmoil in others and driven to try to fix it. It exhausted him and played hell with his romantic relationships.

Some people also become the designated feeler for the family, tasked with the job of expressing and cycling through their emotions on the surface, sometimes loudly, by siblings or parents who couldn't process their own feelings as fluidly or easily.

Kids in this role can take a lot of flak for seeming out of control, when in fact they are acting as emotional hazard cones, troubling reminders to everyone else that feelings are important and real and always present, no matter how much there might be a conspiracy to ignore them. I was one of those people.

Some people are sensitive enough to what's going on in those around them that they subtly pick up the feeling states of others and take them on as their own without even knowing they're doing it. This can be stressful and mystifying. During my college years, I found solace in the communal kitchen outside my dorm. The quiet space allowed me to delve into my thoughts, while the floor-to-ceiling windows offered a panoramic view of the world outside. I was cocooned in overwhelming sadness and pain, initially without understanding its origin. Melancholy wrapped around me, with inexplicable bouts of tears, leaving me to wonder, *Where is this coming from?* It took a lot of parsing for me to realize that at least some of it was not even mine at all, even if I still felt it as real. I was absorbing the intense emotions of those around me—friends navigating breakups, peers grappling with sleep-deprived stress, and family members confronting serious health issues. This process of inadvertently internalizing others' emotions left me mentally and physically exhausted, yet it also illuminated the vital need for boundaries and self-care around groups of people.

Feeling fully can be inconvenient if you haven't got a place for it. A big crying jag, even if the tears are of appreciation and gratitude rather than sadness or despair, can be physically tiring. It requires some space and time to come back to calm, steady equilibrium. Thankfully, there are some great strategies for safely riding emotional waves that we're going to explore in this chapter.

If you're not experienced with identifying and trusting how you feel, know that this skill can be learned. Whatever your own relationship to emotional states, this chapter exists to demystify them and invite you not to fear them.

I want to add a caveat, however. Some feelings, if they've been ignored or denied for too long, can take on outsize power. Some feelings seem as if they'll never go away. If, in the course of doing shadow work, you find yourself truly overwhelmed, and no technique can help you ground yourself and come to calm, it is important to reach out to another person, like a trusted friend or partner or, if you have the means, a professional therapist. We'll consider when you need to do this in greater detail below.

Like the rest of our mammalian brothers and sisters, humans evolved to be emotional creatures because our complex social structures demanded sophistication for us to thrive. We needed to read subtle cues and develop a more finely tuned sense of well-being for our communities to cohere in the face of predators, rival groups, and other stressors. The importance of human emotions is borne out in the sequence of how our brains develop. The emotional center, known as the limbic system, forms after the reptilian brain, responsible for bodily functions, but before the logical and rational parts start to come online.

The limbic system is a crucial part of the central nervous system that, when a threat or an opportunity is sensed, releases hormones into the bloodstream that trigger feeling states, like a weathervane or a radar sensing beyond us, and projecting out through body cues into our families and communities. To a greater or lesser extent, we all grow up learning to take emotional temperatures. Our brains and hearts and souls evolved based on what we got back. "If you feel safe and loved, your brain becomes specialized in exploration, play and cooperation; if you are frightened and unwanted, it specializes in managing feelings of fear and abandonment," writes Bessel van der Kolk, MD, in *The Body Keeps the Score: Mind, Brain and Body in the Transformation of Trauma*.[4] This is an echo of Jung in a different language. For Jung, emotions and traumatic memories that were pushed into the shadow often resurfaced as complexes or psychological disorders.

Not everyone who does shadow work is dealing with major trauma, but the insight gained from trauma research has implications for emotional processing in general. For shadow work to root deeply, it must include body awareness and bring the body into the process.

Peter Levine theorized that under traumatic conditions—physical, emotional, or sexual abuse; car accidents and other physical injuries; even humiliating moments in public with no escape—the body needs to take meaningful action to flee, fight back, or hide. It is when there are no means to do so that traumatic injuries follow. In the book *In an Unspoken Voice: How the Body Releases Trauma and Restores Goodness*,[5] Levine recounts the experience of being hit by a car while walking in his neighborhood. Using knowledge gleaned from his own research, he was able to monitor his physical responses, breathe deeply, find a calming witness, and allow his body to tremble and shake in the aftermath—all techniques that allowed his heart rate to return to a normal level sooner so he could avoid developing PTSD.

Trembling and shaking after a shocking episode are "ways the nervous system 'shakes off' the last rousing experience and 'grounds us' in readiness for the next encounter with danger, lust and life," Levine writes.[6] They are animal and instinctual responses, "mechanisms that help restore our equilibrium after we have been threatened or highly aroused. They bring us back down to earth, so to speak."

This is a specialized, clinical way of describing how I would get myself out of states of heightened anxiety when I was younger and suffered from panic attacks. At the dance studio, snarky looks and bullying whispers isolated me, making each class a dreaded ordeal. Just ten minutes before class, I would hide in a bathroom stall, desperate to escape the others. In the quiet of that stall, I began to explore my anxiety. One day, to shake off the overwhelming fear, I started jumping in the stall. Jumping turned into jumping jacks. Relief! I felt so much relief. The physical movement allowed me to release the stress through my body, gradually helping me build enough courage to show up in the studio more fully.

This technique became a lifeline, helping me cope not just with dance class but also with other anxiety-inducing situations that developed later in my life. Whether it was school or random triggers that surfaced, those moments of physical exertion in the bathroom stall taught me how to reclaim my sense of control.

Even if you undergo a disturbing experience that doesn't qualify as major trauma, if you are not able to ground your body by moving, breathing, and recentering your awareness, your "resilience, sense of OK-ness and belonging in the world have been diminished," writes Levine.[7] This same wisdom applies when revisiting painful memories, which in extreme cases can be somatically reexperienced at the same time.

Van der Kolk and Levine focus mostly on trauma, but more generally, they present two of the most intelligent, concrete, and complete arguments that the esoteric, woo-woo idea of body intelligence, a phrase you might have heard in a yoga class and then forgotten, is a fundamental, scientific truth, backed up by tens of thousands of hours of clinical research.

This has great implications if you are someone who has a hard time accessing your emotions or understanding them. An awareness of your body, which is so much easier to cultivate, is your golden ticket to gaining clarity on your feelings. Knowing when you are troubled and where in your body you feel it and developing the instinct to breathe and ground when you're triggered are crucial steps in gaining emotional maturity that happen step by step and get stronger and more solid over time. Focusing on your body with curiosity as it experiences emotional states also takes you out of overly moralizing your experiences, which is key when accessing your shadow.

An awareness of your body, which is so much easier to cultivate, is your golden ticket to gaining clarity on your feelings.

Keep in mind that when people talk about embodiment, there are generally two types. The first is when you're triggered, threatened, feeling adrenaline, vigilance, or pain. This could be from a firsthand experience or remembering one. The fight-or-flight reflex is triggered in your amygdala, deep inside your limbic brain. This is the kind of sensation that Levine and van der Kolk would counsel benefits from physical expression to discharge in the moment. The second, which is one of the goals of successful shadow work, is when you're peacefully aware of your body in all that you do. When you're "in your body," your senses are more available, and your wiser, calmer self is in the driver's seat. This kind of awareness doesn't come from stress, it helps relieve it.

Therapies like EMDR and Brainspotting, which both engage the field of vision as part of healing trauma and include memory, visualization, and emotion, use both kinds of body awareness. I consider them both as types of shadow work. In a typical session, a therapist will ask their patient to turn to their body to confirm what material needs to come up for healing. Usually this happens by thinking of the core issue and placing attention on the location and level of their physical agitation at the same time. They're asked to target and describe the feeling on the somatic level with no attachment to the story of how it got there: maybe it's butterflies in the stomach, or a sense of tension around the neck and shoulders. After some grounding protocols, the patient then either moves their eyes back and forth in rapid succession while replaying the traumatic memory (in EMDR) or focuses on a fixed point in space (in Brainspotting) while letting the mind wander into active imagination, in both instances being asked to stay in awareness of physical sensation throughout. Right before the session is over, the patient compares their present level of agitation to how they felt at the start of the session, to gauge its effectiveness and help the therapist navigate further treatment.

NAMING AND UNDERSTANDING YOUR EMOTIONS

At this point it's worth getting a little more specific on individual emotions themselves. Unscientifically, based on my own experience and what I've learned from speaking to journalers and experts, I'm including a list of the most common ones that arise when people first start to do shadow work. Most of the time, these feeling states are transitory and relatively harmless when you know how to carry them.

Next, you'll find a list of the most common emotions you experience as you make progress, followed by some tips on how to pinpoint and navigate through the tough stuff. I've categorized both lists by whether the emotion sits high on the emotional vibration scale or low, and whether it tends to be generally light or dense in the body. In the Zenfulnote app, this structured approach is part of the emotion check-in form and is designed to support you in tracking your emotional journey with clarity and intention. This categorization helps you quickly recognize the nature of how you feel and understand its impact on your well-being.

Nothing here is mutually exclusive. No matter where you are in life, you will wind your way through most of these emotions at some point. Keep in mind that my definitions may not be yours. The places in my body I'm mentioning that correspond to my emotional states may not correspond to yours. You may find completely different results. If so, that's great! I encourage you to make your own map, write your own definitions, and treasure them.

SCAN HERE

Download Zenfulnote

Common Emotions That Arise When Starting Shadow Work

A. APPREHENSION

(Low vibration, dense)

Future-projecting, expecting the negative, even the worst. I often feel it as butterflies in my stomach or tightness around my neck and shoulders.

B. ANNOYANCE OR IRRITATION

(Low vibration, dense)

The short fuse, the sharp, instant reply, can be like a snakebite to anyone in its path. When you're managing internal and external conflicts, irritation often strikes. It feels high-wire and electric to me and comes with tension around my eyes and forehead.

C. JEALOUSY

(Low vibration, dense)

Either simmering or on full boil, jealousy is feeling unbalanced over how someone else feels or spends their time, which are matters that are usually outside your control. This feeling, which I usually feel in the pit of my stomach, comes coupled with a sense of being insulted, overlooked, misunderstood, and unseen. The mental churn connected to jealousy needs to find peace as much as the bruised heart.

D. GENERALIZED STRESS OR OVERWHELM

(Low vibration, dense)

You don't know why you're so exhausted, or your resources so low. Maybe your mind is working on five levels at once, and you feel like you're one step away from crashing. You can't bring all of yourself to anything because you're so all over the place. This can be a smokescreen to avoid focusing on something you don't want to look at, but it's also an important gauge of how much gas you really have in your tank, so, as with all these emotional responses, don't blow it off or wave it away.

E. ANXIETY

(Low vibration, dense)

You feel like a rabbit being chased by hounds. The world is moving too fast, your thoughts are racing, along with your breath and heart. There might be a gnawing feeling in your stomach, and you might feel dizzy too. Even if some part of you knows an anxious thought process isn't real, the rest of you gets caught up in it anyway. Memories can often cause anxiety in the present, as can projecting your attention too far into the unknown future. I have suffered a lot of anxiety in my life.

F. DREAD

(Low vibration, dense)

A sense of impending doom, dark and foreboding. Something terrible is out there in the future, just out of reach, both mysterious and familiar at the same time. I feel this one in my feet, in my stomach, and in my heart and throat.

G. SADNESS

(Low vibration, dense)

A bottomless well of tears that threatens to overflow. The heart aches, whether for yourself or for someone else. Sadness is profound, but it is also soft. It hangs around my neck and shoulders and heavy in my heart.

H. ANGER

(Low vibration, dense)

It's crispy, it's hot, it's kinetic and fiery. It is often socially unwelcome, from women especially. Anger feels like one of the hardest emotions to contain in the body. In an ideal world it needs yelling, pillow punching, or growling to get it out. Some people carry it inside them their whole lives, the incentive to ignore it is so great. It is a challenging one to feel safe with, but if expressed responsibly, it is powerful, like a snorting, bucking bronco worth learning to ride.

I. DISAPPOINTMENT

(Low vibration, dense)

Sigh. This again. It always happens like this. . . . When events or people don't live up to my ideals, it feels like three hundred extra pounds on my shoulders. Breath comes slowly. Colors lose their intensity. Tears well up. I am six years old again, and someone forgot to pick me up from school. I feel small and rueful because it's a feeling based on negative familiarity. When you do shadow work, it's exceptionally common to revisit disappointments you felt when you were young.

J. FEAR

(Low vibration, dense)

This one is impossible to ignore. Your heart rate goes up, your stomach rumbles, you might physically shake. It's another future-projected emotion, often called up based on projections buttressed by lived experience. For many it's so intolerable they turn to substances to turn down the volume. Fear can be one of the harder emotions to allow yourself to feel without self-criticism, if what you fear seems out of proportion to events, or if you're used to being tough and independent. It's okay. Most people experience some form of fear almost every day. While that fear can be limiting, it can also be lifesaving.

K. RESENTMENT

(Low vibration, dense)

In doing shadow work, you may develop a new understanding of how you have been treated in the past. Getting clear on how someone has hurt you, maybe repeatedly, means passing through resentment. It's anger and discontentment directed at someone close that you often keep covert for the sake of peacekeeping. Unrecognized, it can poison close relationships. Recognized, it can be cleared.

Common Emotions That Result from Doing Shadow Work

A. JOY

(High vibration, light)

This one is best when it sneaks up on you, though I'll take it anytime. It's buoyant laughter, lightness, effervescence, bouncing, fluttering. It's a puppy when its person comes home. I found joy in surprising places after I started doing shadow work, most often in nature. I feel joy like a wave of bright golden light that goes through me from head to toe.

B. ALIVENESS

(High vibration, light)

This is the steady hum of a thriving organism. You're switched on, ready and in an easy, cruising gear. I recognize aliveness when I can feel the energy in my hands and feet, and my heart feels content, and I am curious and alert. Often, I find myself laughing more easily.

C. PLAYFULNESS

(High vibration, light)

When your inner child is seen and heard and respected, this precious feeling is much more abundant. In moments of play, we lose our sense of time, letting go of inhibitions and becoming fully immersed in the joy and wonder of the present.

D. HOPEFULNESS

(High vibration, light)

Like disappointment, this is both a mental state and a feeling one. It's born of faith and an openness to the unknown. It came more readily to me when I started seeing myself responding to triggers differently. I started to believe in positive possibilities in a way that I could feel in my bones.

E. CURIOSITY

(High vibration, light)

When we are centered and whole, we are naturally curious. Curious about other people and their experiences, curious about parts of ourselves we have yet to know. This sense of wonder keeps us engaged with life, always eager to learn and evolve. It builds on itself.

F. PASSION

(High vibration, light)

When we're not spending so much time white-knuckling through pain, we have a lot more available energy to engage with the things that rev us up. I regained many lost passions from doing shadow work and formed new ones. This book is one of the results.

G. COMPASSION

(High vibration, light)

The extension of love and understanding to yourself or to another. Compassion is rich and warm, like honey. It facilitates intimacy and connection and healing like little else.

H. ANGER (THAT IS NOW OWNED AND ACCEPTED AND APPROPRIATELY DIRECTED)

(High vibration, dense)

Yes, our sometimes-inconvenient friend shows up on this list too. When anger is acknowledged, accepted, and given its proper place, like in response to a real injury, it can be a righteous protector. Appropriate anger can help you set crucial boundaries and stand up for yourself.

I. CONTENTMENT

(High vibration, light)

Sometimes I look around me and take stock of what I've been able to overcome and build, and I just feel glad to be alive. I'm not trying to get more more more, I'm simply good, right here, right now. Contentment feels like a belly full of warm oatmeal and the smell of my mother's perfume.

J. GRATITUDE

(High vibration, light)

This emotion is a life-extender like nothing else. When I make a list every morning of what I'm grateful for, I feel a spark in my heart and a glow that extends outward into the room.

There are many creative ways to find your way through the wild, sometimes unfamiliar fields of all these feelings. Let's start with the basics of how to handle upsetting triggers, informed by van der Kolk's and Levine's imperatives. Deep belly breathing is the number one go-to for all states of upset. If your heart is racing, try to make your exhale longer than your inhale. Ideally you get so used to doing this that it becomes a reflex, and you start doing it naturally when you are distressed. If you don't have a practice currently where you do it every day, establish one, even if it's only setting a timer and belly breathing with your eyes closed for five minutes.

Deep belly breathing is the number one go-to for all states of upset.

Alfred, twenty-nine, from just west of Dallas, is neurodivergent and found dance to be a crucial component in accessing and expressing his emotions. "If somebody asked me before, moving emotions through my body was near impossible," he recalls. "It was like this huge, huge wall, because if I couldn't intellectualize something, I couldn't understand it. Dance really liberated me, because I could exist in any energy I wanted. It deepened my relationship with different raw energies within me, things I couldn't verbalize or conceptualize concretely. It had a cascading effect with how I interacted with myself and expressed myself. I was an athlete before, but I could dance really close to my heart. I feel like that brought out something very primal and raw in me."

Lawrence found a similar trail to effective shadow work through meditation and running. When he divorced at age thirty and got laid off from a high-performance job at the same time, he realized that sessions with his therapist needed to be supplemented with a deep, solo inner journey. As someone who suffered from anxiety made worse by years of abusive bullying in junior high and high school, "I don't think I could have done it if I didn't know how to ground myself first," he says. "When I was younger, I'd go from being shoved against lockers and having bottles of water emptied onto my head, to going into English class all wet and having to pretend like it didn't happen. I had to compartmentalize and just get good grades. I never learned how to feel my feelings. I never learned how to cry. I could cry watching a sad movie, but I never just sat and cried. It almost felt as if the emotional pipes in my body were not flowing. I was suppressing a ton, smoking so much weed. The high feeling clogged the parts of me that I needed to listen to the most."

Lawrence started meditating before he would do his daily journaling. "Things were so heavy for me, and I had to get to a place mentally where I wasn't just thinking about a thousand things at once." In addition to the calm, steady breathing that accompanied his mindfulness practice, he trained for a marathon and used guided meditations from Headspace that came with his membership in the Nike Run Club app. They encouraged a similarly mindful approach to his body as he put one foot in front of the other every day. "There was this voice literally coming through the headphones saying, 'How are you feeling right now in this moment?'"

As his mind-body awareness deepened, Lawrence started a morning practice that he continues to do every day. "As soon as I wake up, I take my journal, put the date at the top of the page and then I write, 'I feel ________' and just sit for a second and try to physically feel my emotions. It might start with, I feel sad, and then any other feelings I could sense in my body, no matter how contradictory they seemed. And then I'd say, 'I think it's about this,'" and he'd allow himself to free-associate. From there, he could start his day from a position of emotional awareness and acceptance.

The exercise that drama coach Julianna Rees mentioned in the previous chapter is worth diving into in this context, because it's one that anyone, acting student or not, can use to get a more 360-degree view and consciously embodied experience of their emotions. It's a little more structured and detailed than Lawrence's morning journaling, but it's in the same spirit. Rees describes it like this:

"I ask my students to identify for themselves where each one feels an emotion, for example, grief or sadness or jealousy or shame, in their bodies. One emotion at a time. Close your eyes, breathe deeply, shut out the outside noise, and turn on your sensors. Maybe it's the throat, or the stomach, or somewhere else.

"Then I'll say, 'OK, that place, is it hot? Is it cold? Does it feel metallic?'" They keep going until each student can clearly describe the emotion in question objectively, using the most descriptive language possible. "You're getting them to be able to sit inside of a really distressing feeling and understand it in all of its crystalline complexity," she explains. Your purpose in doing this exercise isn't to perform or reproduce emotions like Rees's students. But it is a great way to map and create a detailed and visceral inventory of something that may have just seemed misty or vague before.

Can you associate a sound to it? A taste or color?

Get out some colored pencils and draw pictures of them if you like. Pay attention to the colors you're drawn to. What associations do the emotions have for you?

Whether earthshaking revelations come to you in this process isn't the point. (Though they might.) The point is to slow down, marinate in, and comprehend an emotion inside out with curiosity. As you let your mind make creative, symbolic associations with physical sensations and felt emotions, you start to know that it's safe to explore there without rushing through it.

There are emotions we encounter inside shadow work. Then there are those that come upon us when we're out in the world, doing our thing, a walking target for triggers. If you're falling into distress from any difficult emotion while you're around people or situations where you can't fully express yourself, try to change the scenery. Get outside the classroom or cubicle or party, even if just for a few moments until you're back to better balance. Every day of your life that you've been in the company of other people, somebody has gotten up and left the room, and you most likely didn't give it a second thought. You can almost always take space for yourself without having to make a big deal out of it.

What if you're in emotional distress that is lasting much longer than the moment or longer than a few days in a row? What if doing shadow work throws you into prolonged despair, anger, or fear? An emotional state that persists despite external conditions can be a sign you're unable to regulate on your own.

If you're experiencing something like this, I encourage you to use a journal. To be fair, I encourage everyone to journal, but especially here. Slowing down and forming sentences that are focused on your present feelings can be soothing. But equally importantly, if you notice that you are going to extreme emotional places too often to maintain your present life, you can share what you've been journaling with a friend or a professional for valuable feedback, perspective, and support.

Write whenever you can find the time and space, but especially in the morning and at the end of the day. If you've had a big emotional release that day, ask yourself how you feel now. Do you feel relief, or have you sunk further into misery? If anxiety is a problem for you, at the end of the day, how much time did you spend in panic versus out of it? What do you feel compelled to do after a big emotional plunge? Are you thrown back onto destructive habits—do you want to drink, smoke, numb out, escape? How seriously? How often?

Prolonged anger needs real strategies for containment. Are you acting out physically on yourself, like punching walls or hurting yourself? Or on others, like starting fights or going overboard physically punishing your kids? If you are going into deeper despair, is it consistently getting in the way of work or your connection to others? Have you entertained thoughts of suicide? This is all valuable information to help you discern if you need to seek help. As I explained earlier, I came to shadow work because I was going through a prolonged depression. One reason I was able to engage in this self-inquiry without a therapist is that I have a caring family network and a supportive partner. I am lucky that way.

I was also able to develop compassion and empathy for myself, despite low levels of available serotonin at the time. I want to underline here that you don't have to be a hero. If you are legitimately overwhelmed by the emotions that arise in doing shadow work, if you find yourself experiencing panic attacks or crushing lows that don't subside, put your journal down for a while and reach out. I am an ambassador to the National Alliance on Mental Illness (NAMI), which is an excellent resource for support and guidance. Consider exploring local therapy options, online therapy services, and mental health apps to help you navigate your inner self in real time and find the clarity you need. Remember, seeking help is a sign of strength, not weakness.

We've created many boxes to organize our lives—from cars to buildings, highways to classrooms, textbooks, smartphones, the list goes on. We've prioritized categorizing and systems at the cost of our own unique emotional depth—a huge red flag for Jung as he observed the march of history into modernity in the twentieth century. Meanwhile, corporations bid for our attention every day through advertisements, embedding billboards into our minds, turning our focus into a currency they control. Sometimes we just need to reclaim our time to play. If this notion doesn't come easily or naturally to you, here are some suggestions:

1. Watch the cartoons you loved as a kid or the show you weren't allowed to as a kid: the thrillers, spicy Spanish telenovelas, anything!
2. Eat dessert first.
3. Explore a new genre of music that you haven't listened to before and create an experimental playlist of the gems you find. The guilty-pleasure genres I've added to mine include melodic techno, neoclassical, and organica, which is house music with African and Latin American influence.
4. Celebrate something mundane every day.
5. Collect something random but meaningful to you. Someone on my "for you" page on TikTok collects Pokémon perfume bottles. I love that.
6. Indulge yourself in your home decor. If you can afford the soft bedsheets, the squishy pillow, the hand-carved antique store vase, get them.
7. Take a mental health day from work when you need it.
8. Download a game on your device. One that helps you with memory, attention, and problem-solving. Something that makes your brain stretch.
9. Dance outrageously, even if you're alone in your room. *Especially* if you're alone in your room.
10. Offer a service for nonmonetary reasons. I know people who offer rideshares just to connect with other humans.
11. Plan a solo trip to a place you've always wanted to visit, or if that's a stretch, plan a solo trip to that inviting coffee shop in your town.

Allow yourself to engage in these small, mighty acts of self-expression and exploration. You will see how it gradually reconnects you with your true self. Don't be afraid to explore, feel, and simply be. The steps you take toward embracing your individuality and emotional freedom will allow you to go backward, inward, reversing the direction society has set for you. It's a shift from running away from yourself to running toward yourself. Close your eyes, open your arms, and embrace the full spectrum of what it means to be *you*.

THREE

SHADOW WORK AND SPIRITUALITY

How can I be substantial if I fail to cast a Shadow? I must have a dark side also if I am to be whole; and inasmuch as I become conscious of my Shadow I also remember that I am a human being like any other.

—C. G. JUNG, *MODERN MAN IN SEARCH OF A SOUL*[1]

There is a question I get from time to time: Is shadow work a spiritual practice?

To that I say, it doesn't have to be, though in my experience, doing shadow work will often lead you there. For Jung, spirituality—as opposed to man-made religion with its dogmas and power trips—was a defining question for humanity. "Only if we know that the thing which truly matters is the infinite can we avoid fixing our interests upon futilities, and upon all kinds of goals which are not of real importance," he wrote in his autobiography, *Memories, Dreams, Reflections*. "The more a man lays stress on false possessions, and the less sensitivity he has for what is essential, the less satisfying is his life. He feels limited because he has limited aims, and the result is envy and jealousy. If we understand and feel that here in this life we already have a link with the infinite, desires and attitudes change."[2]

For many people doing shadow work, there does eventually come a sense of being connected to something larger than all of us, something benevolent and life-giving and nurturing. "My mother would be rolling over in her grave if she heard me say this now," says Johnny, whom we met in Chapter One, of his recent passage to spirituality. He was raised religious but never believed it much. He went to church because his mother made him. After undergoing his dark night of the soul a few years ago, which included shadow work journaling and Alcoholics Anonymous, he has started going to church again too. In the softening that came from his shadow work practice, after separating from his wife and no longer living with his kids full-time, he saw a need for fellowship around bigger life questions. The church he chose wasn't the same one as his mother's, but one with an openhearted congregation. "Now, going in with an open mind, I look at it as being softened up, because I've been able to figure me out as a person, and how I operate, and now there's a level of peace I feel there. I go there for a different perspective and understanding."

I want to be clear that you do not have to be in a religious community to benefit from shadow work. You don't have to attend church, go to temple, or pray. Spirituality, as I intend it to mean, is beyond any one discipline or system. It can start with the simple awareness of a loving connection to nature, humanity, animals, trees, the sky, and yourself.

I saw a meme somewhere that read, "A person searching for God is like a fish searching for water." Just as water always surrounds a fish, so too is our spirit always present around and within us, even if we're not always aware of it. What we're seeking is already a fundamental part of our existence.

Spirituality, as I intend it to mean, is beyond any one discipline or system. It can start with the simple awareness of a loving connection to nature, humanity, animals, trees, the sky, and yourself.

Spiritual experiences take many forms: the way your heart cracks open from a mountain view; the wave of liquid joy that comes greeting a new baby; the feeling in your heart you get from embracing an old true friend, or from embracing a tree; a sudden realization that you are surrounded by love. These moments could simply be called joy, except that they also inspire wonder and break time in half, piercing deep into the gut. They operate on a different wordless, feeling plane of existence than the part of us that clock-watches and calorie-counts.

Jung concluded that a person's unique process of individuation—facing and embracing their shadow—is a form of spiritual growth, and that the unconscious in all its forms is a rich source of spiritual insight and wisdom. Without its input, which is made more fluid through shadow work, the life path remains unclear and unsatisfying.

Our quest for meaning is what separates us from the animals, and through that quest comes the chance to find the treasure trove of peace. It's just that the "spirit" in our society is being stripped out through judgment and social conditioning. Jung worried about modern humanity's reliance on materialism, excessive rationality, and hard science, its urbanization and industrialization, and its alienation from the sacred. He felt the contemporary West lacked respect for the body and its natural rhythms, nature in general, and the feminine principle. "As scientific understanding has grown, so our world has become dehumanized," he wrote in *Man and His Symbols*. "Man feels himself isolated in the cosmos, because he is no longer involved in nature, and has lost his emotional 'unconscious identity' with natural phenomena. . . . His contact with nature has gone, and with it has gone the profound emotional energy that this symbolic connection supplied."[3] I see this today in dismissive strangers, online bullying, the relentless pursuit for success at all costs, the pressure to present a perfectly polished, smiling face to the world despite how you might feel inside, and how mental health struggles are stigmatized and shamed.

Everyone has a soul, and they can access it anytime. Anything can be a spiritual practice if it provides an outlet for your soul's growth and nourishment. If you pay attention and explore intentionally—through prayer, meditation, contemplation, tribal dance, openhearted dream analysis, visualization, ritual, yoga, chanting, breath work, or sacred ceremonies—you will hear your spirit calling. Listen to what it says. There are guides and messages within us all, accessible in so many ways. If you remember Lawrence, for him the simple act of running with focused and sustained attention on his emotions and his bodily experience brought him the space to ground and contemplate, while pushing him toward a greater inner strength. Explored with enough depth and intention, almost anything becomes spiritual.

What is it that your soul calls for that you have yet to respond to?

If you allow yourself to consciously open to the divine, or spirit, or the soul, or your inner knowing, or your higher self, or God, or whatever you want to call it, it leads to a more harmonious balance between your inner and outer worlds. Ignoring spirit, its energy must go somewhere. For some, it shows up as physical ailments, compulsive behaviors, depression, and other emotional struggles. Amila, twenty-eight, is the daughter of Bosnian survivors of the Balkan war in the 1990s. She came to America at nine months old and felt split between two cultures most of her young life. She worked hard in school, pushing all her tension, insecurities, and inherited multigenerational trauma to the side. She graduated early and became an English teacher at nineteen, but soon her inner turmoil manifested. "I was very successful, but at the same time, I was battling chronic illness," she recalls. "I was diagnosed with fibromyalgia at twenty, my body was failing me, and I eventually got addicted to painkillers. Depression and anxiety followed." In one particularly dark moment, "I had a gun in one hand and a bottle of pills in the other. I heard the thought, 'I need to go find a body of water.'" She heeded that voice and went to a nearby lake. There, rather than throw herself into the water to drown, she felt the urge to grab a pen and paper. "I heard my thoughts for the first time in a long time," she says. "I sat there for hours journaling."

After this peak experience, Amila entered a period of deep contemplation. She quit her job and spent half a year in full hermit mode. During that period, she paid attention to words and ideas that crossed her path as if by accident, like the word "transcending." She looked it up, and one discovery led to another until she went down the rabbit hole and found shadow work. It helped her connect to her family's unhealed wounds as well as her own.

How often do you contemplate? How will you choose to contemplate?

How often do you contemplate? How will you choose to contemplate?

"The way I like to see it is my higher self, my intuition, was calling," Amila explains, thinking back to that first lifesaving journaling session and the practice of contemplation that followed. "It felt like this wisdom was being poured onto me, not that I suddenly became strong and wise." She interpreted her insightful downloads as channeling from another source, and paid attention to what she learned. (Jung had his own experiences with channeling, in the form of a spirit guide he named Philemon, who first appeared to him in a dream in 1913 and remained a figure of solace and wisdom throughout his life.[4]) As Amila continued to invest in her spiritual experiences and they became a calling, her physical ailments stopped nagging her. Her depression lifted. She decided she wanted to use what she was receiving in her journaling and meditation to help others, and now, alongside running a trucking business with her husband, she is a professional spiritual coach with a thriving practice.

An important aspect of Amila's story is how, even after a transformative awakening, she kept her feet on the ground. Even as her worldview and daily lived experience underwent a radical shift imbued with new purpose, she never cut ties with the supportive people around her who knew her best and acted as her anchors: her husband and her family.

Sometimes when people undergo a spiritual conversion, the temptation can be strong to overthrow absolutely everything in their lives: their families, their jobs, their homes. An extreme example of this is people who join cults or become adherents of totalizing spiritual communities. The dream is that you can remove yourself all at once from your past problems, and even from your shadow, to transcend to a higher plane. That you can entirely reprogram yourself to think only positive thoughts by removing all negative stressors. The technical term for this is "spiritual bypass," and for some people it's a tempting form of escape.

While there is much to be said for adjusting your life to practice more positivity and sustenance—it's a key component of shadow integration, in Chapter Eight—you cannot entirely remove yourself from conflict, crisis, or challenge like a Biosphere 2 tree. You cannot simply wish or pray or positively think triggers away. There will always be darkness in you—it's part of what makes you who you really are. Accepting this and loving yourself for it, even as you work to become more conscious, brings far more lasting peace than fantasies of ascension.

"Part of the issue with the spiritual work as I see it, and especially in the New Age movement, is it doesn't take into account the fact that we have a dark side and we have an animal side," says Rainn Wilson, the actor and author of *Soul Boom: Why We Need a Spiritual Revolution*.[5] "It's the story of the rider and the elephant. Our consciousness is the rider on top of the elephant, but the elephant is much stronger than the rider. The elephant is our desires, our lusts, and really, it's the elephant that's driving us. So, there's a lot of unpacking we need to do around [who we are]. Where am I selfish? What are the secrets that I keep? What are the aspects of myself I like the least? What do I like to keep in the darkness? And how can I benefit from shining a light onto my shadows?"

There is much transcendence to be had here on earth, in the gray areas of the thick of your life, even in such secular spaces as a therapist's office. By some definitions, certainly by Jung's, personal growth and spiritual growth are the same thing, because they lead to greater awareness, strength, and wisdom. In *No Bad Parts: Healing Trauma and Restoring Wholeness with the Internal Family Systems Model*,[6] the psychologist Richard Schwartz, PhD, lays out the theory and practice of Internal Family Systems therapy, a modality that looks at the inner self as a sometimes dysfunctional system of role-playing parts, mostly developed in childhood, that need to be brought into awareness, loved, appreciated, heeded, and understood to be transformed. While building a practice that might have been classified as pure psychology, over time Schwartz realized that "parts work" is essentially spiritual. "I've been developing IFS for almost four decades," he writes. "It's taken me on a long, fascinating—and as emphasized in this book—spiritual journey that . . . has transformed my beliefs about myself, about what people are about, about the essence of human goodness, and about how much transformation is possible."[7]

Seen this way, psychology and spirituality are not opposites but interconnected. The sheer number of Jungian therapists who are also ministers and rabbis is also proof! Therapeutic approaches like Schwartz's (which has been called "Jung plus") provide a holistic path to healing that fosters a sense of meaning, purpose, and connection to all that is.

One thing that shadow work has done for me is decluttered my path, taking away the intensity of triggers and, like Johnny, pointing me to peace, which transformed into a sense of oneness with everything and respect for the great mystery of life. Shadow work has also helped me maintain a happier equilibrium because I'm not looking for perfection or lightness devoid of all dark, so I'm not freaked out when I see darkness in me. I honor it for what it teaches me about myself and where I've come from, and how it shows me what I need to keep working on to heal.

Shadow work has also helped me maintain a happier equilibrium because I'm not looking for perfection or lightness devoid of all dark, so I'm not freaked out when I see darkness in me.

In that way, I am, and anyone else doing shadow work is, a link in a long chain. Indeed, as long as there have been humans, there have been human spirituality, ritual, and the quest for meaning and balance. Evidence goes back to the Paleolithic era, with discoveries of the burial of human dead.[8] It had social-spiritual meaning because burial, much less ceremonial treatment of corpses, was something our animal friends never bothered with. In some cave paintings of the first humans, there were pictures of animals they didn't hunt, revealing a symbolic connection to other forms of life.[9]

Spirit has been central to the human experience ever since. Rituals and cults formed everywhere around death and fertility, the end and the beginning of all life, which necessarily entails pain, darkness, and fear. Before Christianity, such challenging states were not seen as evil, but rather as another face of the divine.

Life is a ceremony,
unfolding in layers like a Russian doll,
Each moment holds the next,
life and death intertwined,
revealing one another in quiet succession.

The oldest-known religious figures, dating back tens of thousands of years, were shamans. "It was the shamans who first emerged on the scene as mediators of the sacred for their people and for purposes of survival and healing," writes the psychologist C. Michael Smith, PhD, in *Jung and Shamanism in Dialogue: Retrieving the Soul, Retrieving the Sacred.*[10] Across Asia, the Americas, Australia, Polynesia, Africa, and Europe, shamans were the first known religious figures, and also the first known shadow workers.

Not all indigenous spiritualities are alike. Not all shamanic traditions are either. But there are enough commonalities across the important distinctions to offer a definition: shamans were initiates who used spiritual powers to intercede on behalf of their fellow humans. With the help of music and trance, and sometimes sacred hallucinogenic plants, they called on spirit allies to restore balance and health to individuals and their larger community. Illnesses, often conceptualized as malevolent spirits, had to be faced and known to be diagnosed and defeated, for the sufferer to be made whole again. Nature and its rhythms and symbols were central to these supernatural practices.

It wasn't just physical sickness that was treated but soul sickness as well—before the arrival of the Enlightenment and our modern notion of medical science, the body and the soul weren't seen as all that separate anyway. (And in many Eastern systems today, like Ayurveda and traditional Chinese medicine, they still aren't.) Depression, anxiety, mourning, the crushing sadness of loss—like Amila, anyone who has suffered them knows how they sap life force as much as many physical diseases. Ancient cultures had different words for these states of being. They defined them as coming from different origins than the paradigms we have today in the West. But they felt the calling of their hearts as surely as we do. And they looked to powerful spiritual elders to help heal them.

Not all this discussion belongs solely to the past. Shamanism continues to thrive today, both in traditional cultures that have survived Western colonialism and among seekers from diverse backgrounds who have embraced what is now often called neo-shamanism. This modern revival has been growing in popularity internationally since the 1960s.

In shamanic cultures, the shaman's initiation is a vital prerequisite—a spiritual quest that involves a metaphorical death and rebirth, emerging with powerful otherworldly allies to guide them. This rite of passage often entails isolation from their community for a solitary journey that could last years. During these vision quests, whether in the darkest heart of the forest for the druids, inside a mountain cave like the Hindu sadhus, in a hut off a tributary of the Amazon in Peru, or on the plains of the desert in the American Southwest, the initiate faces their greatest fears—the essence of shadow work. They might experience an imaginary dismemberment of their spiritual body, only to be reassembled in a more masterful form. Often, sacred hallucinatory plants they ingest induce terror that they must confront and conquer.

"In that transformative or death/rebirth experience, the shaman learns what he or she fundamentally *is*, what his or her deepest wounds are, and how to heal or bind them up," writes Smith. "It is as a result of these discoveries, teachings and healings that the shaman gains the wisdom, vision and power to see into the souls of other afflicted individuals, to diagnose and treat them by the power of, and under the direction of, the spirits."[II] Their new spiritual power, the result of harrowing personal trial, was to be put to use for the good of the people. This might include helpful techniques that were revealed to them by their plant teachers or under trance.

Jung wasn't a shaman, nor did he have an in-depth understanding of shamanic practices, despite his fascination with them. Overextending this metaphor would dilute its meaning, and I respect the specific lineages of shamanic paths too much to do that. However, it's hard to disagree with Jung's broad conclusion that modern humans have much to learn from these wounded healers who engage with the forces of light and dark to tend to the health of both body and soul.

"Oh yes, shamanism is all about shadow work," says Benjamin Bernstein. He has lately been revisiting the diaries he kept during his initiations, which mostly took the form of ayahuasca ceremonies. "There can be tremendous physical tension, all kinds of discomfort can happen. I've done ceremonies where I literally shook for hours as the medicine went through. If you need to shit fire, or holler and cry, fine. You have to surrender to the medicine and let it have its way with you." Over and over again, over three hundred times and counting, he cleared resistance and personal demons, and peeled off layers of received wisdom that didn't comport with who he was discovering he was.

He did this after twenty years on a spiritual path that was much more about light, without the intense self-inquiry of shadow work. But after two decades on that path, he felt that his emotions were shut down and knew he needed to go into the dark inside to reclaim them. First, he studied Vipassana meditation, which asks practitioners to see everything inside them and sit with it in a space of nonjudgment. "This practice opened my heart," he says. He then tried taking plant medicine, at first for his own spiritual benefit. Only after undergoing multiple ceremonies did he feel the call to become a shaman himself. Today he doesn't lead others in plant ceremonies, but he guides clients through their own shadow work, sometimes using the Internal Family Systems method, which he calls "shamanic soul retrieval by another name."

In removing ourselves from the cycles of nature, denying our carnality, and going without direct spiritual experiences, Jung believed that Western society underwent a dangerous psychic split that gave evil much greater destructive power. Jung was a witness to two world wars, the rise of fascism, and the creation of the atom bomb, history-shaking developments that changed humanity forever—it's no wonder he thought the way he did about the Western shadow and its turbocharge. "We must beware of thinking of good and evil as absolute opposites," he wrote in *Memories, Dreams, Reflections*. "Recognition of the reality of evil necessarily relativizes the good, and the evil likewise, converting both into halves of a paradoxical whole."[12]

In removing ourselves from the cycles of nature, denying our carnality, and going without direct spiritual experiences, Jung believed that Western society underwent a dangerous psychic split that gave evil much greater destructive power.

Luckily, just by being human, we have the inherent ability to heal this split if we are willing. So far, I've talked about the shadow as a personal repository for an individual's suppressed qualities, desires, and abandoned gifts. While each person's shadow is unique—shaped by their upbringing, family, and cultural context—the existence of the shadow itself is a universal human experience.

But we have much more in common than just that all of us have our own shadow and our own souls. Buried beneath our own individual psyches, which include our conscious and unconscious parts and our individual shadows, rests a more ancient territory that harkens back to humanity's earliest beginnings, which we all have access to. Jung called this the collective unconscious, and it was one of his most radical and meaningful propositions. It means we are much more alike than we are different. It means that in the deepest recesses of our DNA, none of us is truly alone.

According to Jung, the human collective unconscious first formed in our earliest prehistory, part of the inherited structure of the human brain. It is the seat of primordial images and instincts that all humans share. In a lecture he delivered in 1936 (later reprinted in *The Archetypes and Collective Unconscious*), he said: "In addition to our immediate consciousness, which is of a thoroughly personal nature and which we believe to be the only empirical psyche (even if we tack on the personal unconscious as an appendix), there exists a second psychic system of a collective, universal, and impersonal nature which is identical in all individuals. This collective unconscious does not develop individually but is inherited. It consists of pre-existent forms, the archetypes, which can only become conscious secondarily and which give definite form to certain psychic contents."[13]

Our fear of the dark goes here, which ties back to the days before humans were apex predators and depended on vision for survival. Our fear of fire, too. These were some of the earliest self-preservation instincts. And our sense of the sacred goes here, as well as many of our most universal human myths and archetypes. We may act out these mythic identities and stories in our own lives without even knowing it. When made conscious and consciously engaged, archetypes that might have once been compulsive can serve as inspiring sources of healing, a subject we'll explore in the following chapter.

By its nature, the unconscious, whether personal or collective, is difficult to study in a lab. But researchers have landed on a few quantifiable findings that may be edging toward it. In *The Presence of the Past*, the biologist Rupert Sheldrake proposes that memory is a capacity that is found in all of nature.[14] Common to all members of a given species is something called their morphic resonance, which connects past and present for all beings of their type. Each rat or sperm whale or iguana taps into a collective storehouse unique to their biology, which includes a kind of species memory. But where it really gets wild: if rats in London today learn a new skill, their species-mates halfway around the world will more easily learn that capacity as well. Most of the laws of nature are more like habits, Sheldrake explains.

Modern religions are filled with rituals around birth and marriage and death, around forgiveness and penance and pilgrimage. But the mere fact of belonging to a religion or partaking in a religious ritual doesn't necessarily make a person healthy or whole. There is a lot of going through the motions in your average house of worship. Like Johnny as a kid, not everyone is there by choice.

Religion's capacity for forgiveness and fellowship can be sustaining, but its cruel face—judgmental, authoritarian, power-tripping, exploitative, abusive—is the source of deep soul wounds for many. Religion can help facilitate transcendence. It can also create more shadow material than it heals.

"My family was bifurcated," says Rainn Wilson, who grew up a member of the Baha'i faith. "Baha'is are very open to the idea that all religious faiths come from a divine source. I had a family that was very open to new ideas and ancient ones. We had many books about Hinduism, Sufism, Sikhism, the Bhagavad Gita, Buddhist ideas, the Vedas and Upanishads. They weren't just sitting on our shelf collecting dust, they were referenced a lot. But at the same time, my family was extremely dysfunctional and unhappy. There was a lot of stress and anxiety and rage and passive-aggressiveness. So here we were having all of these conversations about transcendence, peace and love, and there was almost zero transcendence, peace and love to be found in the family household. That creates a colossal mindfuck for a kid. Like, we're going to talk about peace, joy, love and happiness, but we're not going to experience peace, joy, love and happiness."

I had a different experience of the shortcomings of organized religion. Growing up in Kingwood, Texas, where the woods met Houston's highways, my parents were pure and kindhearted spirits deeply rooted in their Catholic faith. Their unwavering love and devotion to each other and their religion inspired my younger brother and me to seek God in our struggles, find meaning in our pain, and share unconditional love with those around us.

Entering adolescence, my perspective on the world expanded, and I began to resist the pressure to conform. At church social events, I started to see how not everything was as holy as my parents were. Boys made sexual jokes, flirtatious remarks, and inappropriate advances, so I felt shame about my body and believed I had to hide my femininity to be respected and heard. I started to see the flaws in the church, feeling the sacredness slipping away from it. We strove for perfection, and it remained elusive, so rather than abandon the idea of perfection, we strove even harder, always frustrated and incomplete.

Learning this lesson from my upbringing, like Wilson has, I started to focus on preserving the sacredness and not allowing the flaws of religiosity to taint my heart against the divine. I was grateful that the rosary taught me meditation and sustained contemplation, and confession instilled in me the practice of self-inquiry. Attending mass showed me the value of being part of a spiritual community. The Eucharist introduced me to the power of ritual. The Bible taught me to seek meaning in symbols beyond their literal context. Still, I knew I needed to grow beyond these confines, to find something freer, more connected to nature, and more original to me.

Some of the people I've come to know in the Zenfulnote community have also had traumatizing experiences of religion, where they have felt condemned, or were even ostracized, for asking questions or straying from the prescribed path. Part of their shadow work journey has included facing the shame and guilt inherited from those rigid structures and forgiving the part of themselves that bought into them. Part of it has been reclaiming the sacred for themselves, on their own terms.

Others have found their purpose in heart-centered ministry and religious community and incorporate shadow work into their calling. Much depends on the space that a particular spiritual path or practice or cleric holds for shadow material, human weakness, and acceptance and forgiveness rather than condemnation.

"In my former religion," says Josh, whom we met in Chapter One, "I felt guilty for almost everything, from how I dressed and ate, to what I watched, was interested in, even where I lived. I was always fighting those feelings and telling myself that putting away those bad parts of myself was for a better life and a future in the next one." Josh came to his religious community ten years ago via marriage, then converted and became a missionary. But some years later, when he started to question his religion's beliefs and culture, he was criticized and shunned. Eventually he and his wife both stepped away from their faith, though they didn't abandon a spiritual path.

When Josh started doing shadow work, "My beliefs were very in flux, and I didn't know what to hold on to," he says. "I didn't believe in some of the doctrines of my faith, and I wasn't sure who God was." In meditation, he encountered the part of himself that still cleaved to his former religion, which he discovered he was still doing battle with. "I realized that person is still a part of me and, misguided as he was, he was doing it out of love, trying to add goodness to the world."

In Josh's journey to acceptance of himself, even the part that fell prey to a high-control religious community, the intensity of the trigger of religion has eased up for him. He can live and let live more easily, a conscious part of his present spiritual path, which is no longer centered on any particular diet—though he did remain vegetarian as his former religion practiced—fixed prophecy, or style of dress. No group can take his sense of the divine away from him. Much of his shadow work path has been to reshape and reframe it, free from coercion or rites that he realized were meaningless to him.

The support and guidance offered by a compassionate and trustworthy cleric can be an excellent setting for shadow work. Kohn, forty-three, became a youth pastor at age eighteen, but he took a creative approach to spiritual inquiry, exploring material beyond the Bible. He was aware it wasn't the only truth out there, and while he stayed within the Christian mainframe, he refused to be dogmatic and followed his curiosity and his heart.

"It was through the experience of exploring what God was that I found myself asking who I was. I was already doing a form of shadow work by always questioning how I showed up." Now he does shadow work in live streams online. He works to break down concepts like mirror work, which wasn't an easy cultural match for everyone in a doctrinal community where there were taboos around mirror gazing, seen as sinful. "The eyes are the window to the soul," he says. "And we believe that when we look at and engage with other people. I posed the question to the community: 'Have you ever gazed into your window?'"

In a spirit of openness and forgiveness, Kohn helps guide congregants through rough patches. They report to him that they are experiencing greater intimacy, forgiveness, and connection as a result.

I mentioned many different ways to connect with spirit earlier in the chapter, but I want to return to the importance of ritual. "Through ritual, we essentially tell our unconscious that we are listening to it," writes Robert Amacker, a shaman and Taijiquan master in the essay "The Reluctant Shaman Returns."[15]

I highly recommend creating rituals anytime, but particularly for doing shadow work. Starting in a ritualistic fashion creates a respectful setting. It sacralizes self-inquiry and provides an important psychic container for traveling through some of the emotionally wilder territory of the personal and collective unconscious. It gives those moments of encounter with the deeper self their proper place and time. When the ritual has ended, you return to "normal life," as you must always do.

I highly recommend creating rituals anytime, but particularly for doing shadow work.

Ritual can be as simple as getting down on your knees to pray or turning off notifications and lighting a candle before journaling or meditating. It can be as complex as a fire walk. We'll finish this chapter with some tips for how to build your own.

There are countless ritual traditions you can take part in, and you can take them with you too. In "Reflections on Thirty-Six Years of Participation in Lakota Sioux Sweat Lodge Ceremonies," the Jungian analyst Dennis Merritt writes about his experience of the purification rite and how he transports it into other spaces. The sweat lodge ceremony, called Inípi in the Lakota language, comprises a series of prayers that take place inside a dark, dome-shaped structure heated by a pit of burning stones, like the womb of Mother Earth herself. That setting and the ritual prayers that take place inside it "[help] create a sense of being an integral member of a community of beings, organic and inorganic, in a way that nourishes and heals the soul," he says.[16]

Merritt, who turned eighty in 2024, has spent almost half his life taking part in Lakota sweat lodge ceremonies. As an analyst, he brings them symbolically into his practice by creating an imaginary sweat lodge with patients, as a psychic safe space to shelter difficult moments, like when a patient experiences a turbulent contact with their shadow. "One experiences the important therapeutic aspects of the container and a center and centering energy through the symbolism associated with the sweat lodge that, together with the ritual and songs, creates an embodied sense of the classical archetypal elements of earth, air, fire and water."[17]

Nature is present in this construction through symbols, a reminder that as we breathe in and out, even if we're on the thirty-sixth floor of a skyscraper in the middle of a city, we are part of a greater intelligence and design. Our problems are anchored in their appropriate context, not diminished as too small, but explored as part of a continuous and rich human lineage. There is strength and inspiration here.

One word Jung used with some frequency was "numinous." The word was coined in 1917 by the German theologian Rudolf Otto, who was looking for a way to define holiness, sacredness, divinity, and intangibility without religious connotations or moral judgment. Numinous experiences are ineffable, hard to put into words, and defy rational consciousness. They are feelings, not disembodied concepts. They happen *to* you. They can't be controlled.

Even if they are not guarantees, rituals are invitations to numinous experiences. "Rituals enable transition from one state of consciousness to another state," says Hans van Wechem, MD, cofounder of the Experiential Training Institute in Amsterdam, which leads therapeutic high-dose psilocybin retreats.* "They have been neglected for such a long time."

On retreats, van Wechem and his partner Jeanine Souren, a psychologist and sexologist, work with participants from a variety of cultural backgrounds, and group ritual is one way to unite them. "We call it opening the field," says Souren. At the

---

* Psilocybin is illegal in the United States and is classified as a Schedule 1 substance under the Controlled Substances Act.

beginning of the retreat, "We always open the field by lighting candles. As we light them, we voice our intentions. We acknowledge that we are part of something way bigger than our personal lives, that we all share the same existence. It creates a sense of safety and pays tribute to the big mystery. It is really helpful in opening up. It's a tribal thing."

The institute's goal for participants taking trips—they typically ingest thirty-five milligrams of psilocybin truffles—is that as they travel through visions and into intense emotional states, they can hold up a figurative mirror to their psyche without too much censorship or rationalization. High doses of psilocybin are said to diminish the ego, so the mirror in this setting can see things it might not be able to in a normal unaltered state. That creates space for other parts of the psyche to stand in the light.

Not everyone is disposed to this kind of journey. People suffering from bipolar disorder or psychosis are unable to participate, and screening is required for everyone to make sure they aren't on any kinds of medication with counterindications. A full day of therapeutic preparation takes place the day before, where Souren and van Wechem help participants plot their conscious mind and "ease into encounters with shadow parts," Souren says. Informed by Internal Family Systems, "We help people find parts they suppressed, and prepare them to meet and talk to them. We make a constellation map of them and ask how people relate to each one. You might not like six-year-old you for all sorts of reasons, so you push that one away." Eventually a hierarchy is established that maps how a participant copes to get by.

The following day, participants go inward on their trip, with the aid of blindfolds and music, to experience inner vision for about five hours. Through their mind's eye, they see which parts of themselves show up and what kinds of new conversations can be had. There is no knowing what will happen before it does. Sacred symbols can surface in turbulent visions. Mythical beasts sometimes appear. The individual and collective unconscious blend in a wild dance. During moments of emotional overwhelm, participants are given breathing exercises and whispered words of support and encouragement, coming back to the body and its breath as an anchor. When the effects of the truffles have diminished, they end the day creating artwork.

The following day is dedicated to closing rituals that include group-bonding experiences, and revisiting the map of the self to see how the constellation contours have shifted. "Nine times out of ten, it's changed," Souren says.

Shadow work for Souren and van Wechem holds space for magic. "A mystical experience is an encounter, or a recognition of unconditional love," van Wechem says. "Those who have had those experiences are beyond words and they can only say, it changed my life completely because now I feel that I belong, instead of being separated."

One of the first rituals that I created for myself was when I attended boarding school in high school, because my parents were living abroad for work. Being cut off from them led me to feel alone and abandoned. So I would take a walk outside at night under the moon and talk to it as if it were God, a mature guide that would listen to me in my confusion. I would ask questions, contemplate, weep, and sometimes even howl a yell or loud sigh of release, crying out with emotion or with things that I wanted answered.

Venting to the moon was me rewilding, coming into touch with my untamed womanhood, and finding the omnipresent divine through a walk in nature, the inner voice of my intuition brushing my soul like the wind tapping on my shoulder. I took this dialogue into my college years, too, and still try to make the space and time for this cathartic release today. Playing music became another sacred act for me. I also had a mystical moment of mirror gazing, where I saw an old woman staring back at me. It was unsettling at first, but when I looked again, this time with love and kindness in my eyes, I saw beauty in the lines of her face and understood it was me. This changed the way I saw myself forever after.

Another technique for embodied emotional healing in Benjamin Bernstein's book *Instant Divine Assistance* takes some of the mindfulness and close attention of Julianna Rees's exercise from the previous chapter and adds the intervention of the divine.[18] It's called the Healing Invocation, and it involves locating troubling emotions in the body, focusing on feeling them, and then calling in the higher self to heal them by bathing them in love.

"Many other paths teach to just sit and be with [shadow material] passively," he tells me. "That will work if you have enough time and patience. If you can sit with it long enough, eventually [the pain] will break up and unwind most of the time. But that could take years, and I don't have a year. Your job with this invocation is simply to feel and take a back seat and let the divine do the work," he says. That means that as you drench yourself in the troubling feeling, feeling it all the way through, you call out to your higher self and ask for the toxic energy to dissipate. (The phrase Bernstein recommends is "Maximum healing that serves highest good please.") You don't give any further direction, you just focus on the feeling and ask your higher power to manage the process. Remain focused on the part of the body where the troubling emotion is located and feel what happens. The goal is for the heavy energy to transform into an awakening to bliss. "While healing can happen instantly, it takes as long as it takes," Bernstein says. "The duration depends mostly on how much heavy energy is being released, your intensity tolerance, and how completely you surrender to the process."

Do you have to believe in God for this to work? "The only thing you have to have is a belief that a higher self could be possible," Bernstein says. "Say to yourself, 'I'm going to try this on a contingency basis, with the idea of, Maybe I have a higher self, and let's see what it can do.' Give it a chance to prove itself."

There are infinite kinds of rituals you can create for yourself. Often these are even more powerful, because they come from inside you. Here are a few basic pointers. See them as inspiration or guidelines, but use your own intuition and follow your own desires:

1) Create a sacred space. This can be an altar you set up somewhere in your home, or a special island dedicated to your communion with spirit. It can be temporary, in a quiet corner of a park, when you take a deep breath, close your eyes, and draw a circle of protection around you before you open your journal. Demarcate it with rocks or twigs or leaves for a visual reminder.

2) You are part of nature, and nature is powerful. Let it be your friend and protector as you journey inward. Bring in the four elements of earth, water, fire, and air. Fill a glass of water, put it down next to a crystal or a beautiful stone, add a feather, and light a candle. If you want to release old thoughts or send intentions into the wind by writing them down and setting them on fire, have a fireproof bowl with you.

3) The deepest parts of our minds respond instinctively to symbols and images. If you can't get your hands on actual objects, incorporate pictures: of flowers, trees, mountains, the sun, the moon, evocative or meaningful animals, allies from your family lineage, gods or goddesses who inspire you, the ocean, a rushing river. Pick what you naturally gravitate to. Notice the colors and shapes that speak to you.

4) Have a special notebook or beautiful paper and a pen that feels good in your hand, in a color that speaks to you, for any writing you want to do.

If, however, you would like to try a preexisting ritual—and there's absolutely nothing wrong with that—I invite you to investigate a practice called Quantum Metamorphosis, which was shared with me by Nicole DeMartine. This is a ceremony of intention setting that takes place on the sacred altar of your own heart. Flash the QR code below to be led through the practice step by step.

SCAN HERE

FOUR

A CALL TO QUEST

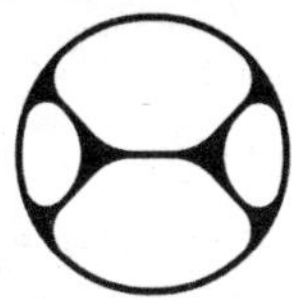

Crazy Horse dreamed and went out into the world where there is nothing but the spirits of things. That is the real world that is behind this one, and everything we see here is something like a shadow from that world.

—BLACK ELK, QUOTED BY JOHN G. NEIHARDT[1]

I see the world as a stage play and often find myself as an observer, sitting quietly in the audience. I'm not alone in this, and I'm sure that many people, perhaps you too, have taken a seat in this grand theater of contemplation. It's comforting to imagine finding Jung, who likely shared this view, a few rows down toward the orchestra pit. Onstage is a moment or memory in your life unfolding. Where are you? Who are you with? What are you acting out? Are you in the throes of a fascination or flooded with deep feeling over the simplest act?

There are times in your life when something jerks you out of the normal flow of events, changes the way you think about and experience yourself, and alters what you thought you came into this life to do. When you know you are at the trailhead of a new path, with a new sense of purpose. It can be entirely self-generated, like when you're visited by an artistic muse you never knew before, and suddenly you want to create and express yourself differently. It can be triggered by another person, like with a strong new attraction that suddenly has you in pursuer mode, when before you might have hung back. A change of self-perception and mission can come from life passages like becoming a parent for the first time. It can also be an addiction or other compulsive new habit with a seeming life of its own that upends how you spend your time and morphs how you show up with others. In Jungian terms, in all these cases, you are in the grip of an archetype—an existential life shift rich with eternal symbolic resonance.

We touched on archetypes briefly in the last chapter when discussing the collective unconscious. Though you may have known the word primarily as a literary term, there is nothing reductive or merely textual in Jung's notion. Archetypes are part of our shared DNA. They're stories and characters and symbols present in dreams, like signposts pointing you to deeper meaning in yourself. Jung defined them as psychic blueprints, or templates, originating from our species' origins, and fueled by our shared humanity over tens of thousands of years. They define critical episodes in the passage of life. As such, they live us as much as we live them. They are not external to us, solely to be perused on an intellectually distant register—though when they are made conscious, archetypes are a fulcrum of power with the potential to be channeled.

You already recognize a lot of archetypes. Fairy tales have long been a repository for them. Many of them are positive: characters like Cinderella, who rises from the ashes to find her true worth, or the Beast, who learns to embrace his humanity, representing universal journeys of growth and self-discovery. Overcoming adversity, embracing the true self, and finding balance between opposing forces—all these archetypal themes are not just entertaining but profoundly instructive, offering insights into possible paths toward individuation and wholeness.

Archetypes are either figures with universal resonance, like the mother, or the wise old man, or they can be symbols, like the cross or the Tibetan mandala (a favorite of Jung's), or whole storylines, like the hero's quest. These eternal characters and narratives captivate us because they reflect our inner struggles and aspirations, providing a mirror to our own journeys of personal growth and the search for meaning in a complex world. By engaging consciously with the archetypes that show up in our lives, we gain deeper insights into who we are and see the intelligence of the patterns that shape our experiences.

By engaging consciously with the archetypes that show up in our lives, we gain deeper insights into who we are and see the intelligence of the patterns that shape our experiences.

The force and sometimes the fury of the unconscious are in play when an archetype moves through you. It's when life calls on you to change in a way that feels destined or bigger than your ego, because it's coming from somewhere much deeper. This can take the form of a voluntary adventure, like a yen to bust out of your routine and go see the world. It can feel like living hell, a destructive drive that causes you to act against the good of your family, like an extramarital affair you can't break off no matter how hard you try because it makes you see yourself as a beguiling lover again rather than an old shoe.

Archetypes usually take hold when it's time to grow and transform. To keep inspiration from becoming obsession, the key is becoming conscious of what's happening. Pay attention when an archetype pops up and you feel a strong pull to it. It could be as simple as your fifty-seventh viewing of *Star Wars*, but this time it really makes you cry. That's your cue to dig deeper inside yourself once you put the remote control back into its box.

The unconscious speaks,
not in words
but in gestures
symbols and clues
Through silently sleeping queues.
It hints at stories
our hearts can't paint.
We watch, we guess, we join the play.

The conscious weeps,
laughs and leaps
and shadows creep
from depths so deep—
A mirror of the mime unseen
reflecting dreams where we have been.

We grasp at threads,
Yet never hold
The fleeting truths
Both shy and bold.
In subtle steps, the mind's ballet,
we move in rhythm, night and day.

The unconscious stirs
in silent streams
through cracks of thought,
in whispered dreams.
It leads us gently by the hand
to places we might understand.

The conscious blinds,
with light so bright,
yet in the dark,
we find our sight.
For in the shadows, softly cast,
we glimpse the future and the past.

So let us dance
this quiet waltz,
between the truths,
between the faults.
For in the mime's soft, silent show,
we find the paths we're meant to go.

Proactively engaging with archetypes is as much a key to becoming your truest and best self as doing shadow work—in fact they work together well. As shadow work brings clarity and understanding about who you really are, the more you do it, the more it helps you engage with the processes and new life phases trying to unfold.

"Until we have given birth to an authentic sense of self, the archetypes are likely to possess us" in their shadow form, explains Carol S. Pearson in *Awakening the Heroes Within: Twelve Archetypes to Help Us Find Ourselves and Transform Our World.*[2] Pearson is also the cocreator of the Pearson-Marr Archetype Indicator, a vetted, peer-reviewed self-assessment tool that helps determine active and unconscious archetypes at work in people and institutions.

When you are in the grip of an archetype unconsciously—when the inner you desperately wants to evolve into a meaningful new role, self-image, or path, but you're not cognitively connecting with that desire—what's happening usually feels like an inner conflict. The part of you that wants to stay the same and the part of you that wants to spread your wings in a different way are like opposing forces waging battle inside you, just outside your daylight view. This can make you feel frustrated, irritable, desperate to escape, bored, depressed, cynical, or just agitated. The best way to move up and out of this state is to address the cacophony and cross-purposes through shadow work. It makes it easier to recognize the deep patterns and urges at work in you and tease out their inherent wisdom to level up intentionally and invest your life with greater meaning.

In this chapter, I'll give you plenty of examples of how people with some experience with shadow work have embraced and moved through an archetypal calling, and I'll outline some techniques to recognize and exchange with these profound symbolic storehouses on your own.

I have heard many stories of shadow work journeys that have followed the contours of initiations, or hero's quests. I know my own first experience with shadow work felt that way to my core. At some point, there comes a sense of mission, enriching and gratifying, suffusing you with faith and excitement, with the feeling that there is a greater intelligence at work. (You already know that I believe there is.) When that comes, the archetypes activated are singing together in harmony, empowering you rather than dragging you down. Like other forms of shadow work, to effectively work with archetypes requires honesty, time, and attention and a willingness to extend yourself the benefit of the doubt.

Your persona is the symbolic mask you wear in society. It is the compass that inspires many archetypes we choose to embody. It's the object that casts your psychological shadow. Think of it as the entry table in a house, adorned with trophies, photographs, degrees, and certifications. The persona is a curated collection of traits you want others to believe define you—a mask that conceals your true self.

The construction of your persona begins early in life, as you discover which aspects of your character gain approval from family and peers and which are rejected. The rejected parts of you are buried behind the mask, into the shadow. Most of us identify with our persona naturally to function and thrive in society. Meanwhile, the shadow resides in the unconscious—a nebulous cloud of forgotten traits, repressed emotions, and unacknowledged pains.

The construction of your persona begins early in life, as you discover which aspects of your character gain approval from family and peers and which are rejected.

Archetypes show that even on the persona level, we're not just one ruling ego, but we have many aspects of our personalities, many stories, many adventures, and take up many roles in life. These available energies play by their own rules, and it's up to us to harness them as best we can. Jung delineated quite a few of them in his writing and analytic practice. Some of the most central include the Self, the divine seat of inner knowing, or the integrated whole being whose ego and unconscious are in healthy balance, centered in the soul. There is the Divine Child, who is healed, evolved, wise, curious, creative, playful, and magical. And, of course, there is the Shadow.

I met my Divine Child after a course of shadow work that had me asking myself what my abandoned passions were. That prompt led me back to creative days when I was younger, in middle school and high school, when I wrote poetry and played music regularly. I mentioned before that I played the flute. I trained first as a hobby, and then it became a true passion: my flute was not just an instrument, but an extension of my soul, like another limb that translated the language of my heart into melody. And then I cut it off once I got to college. Later I realized, in the safety of my diary, where I could admit anything to myself, that I was afraid to let my parents down by not pursuing a career in an industry with a high success rate. It is hard to make a living as a musician, and they didn't think I could. I absorbed their logic as a means of survival, like most kids do.

That realization helped me connect to how, in my adult professional life, on a career path I had by then realized wasn't really mine, I was triggered anytime I heard classical music, especially if it was a piece I used to play on my flute. I remember one evening at a restaurant, when I overheard a familiar song, the confusing wave of joy and sorrow I felt as the melody filled the air. My heart sank, and I withdrew into silence, then sullenness and irritability. This was the Creator in me whom I had rejected, whose conscious loss I hadn't fully grieved, and who refused to just stay asleep.

In continuing my self-investigation, I saw that I was afraid to pick up the flute in my present life, because now I might not live up to my past prowess or be able to rediscover that flow. Where I was tempted to let that part of me remain untarnished, perfect in the untouchable past, because it might be easier, in the here and now, I was clearly in conflict with parts of myself I had tried to kill off and couldn't. So no, denying it wasn't easier.

Eventually, after facing all this potential shame and disappointment in myself, I cleared away the tension and drama around playing music. Today I play regularly, with joy, indulging my inner Creator with ease to the delight of my Divine Child, because I don't need to be the best in the world. I just need to connect with my soul and let the music that lives inside it speak through my precious instrument.

Throughout his writings, Jung fleshed out many archetypes that naturally correspond to life phases, potential journeys, and outlooks—you'll identify with some of them right off the bat. I've chosen ones that recur in his work and in the work of Jungian scholars who have continued to develop his thinking. Each is worth diving into and analyzing on its own for how often it might show up in your life, usually, at first, discontentedly. I promise you it will get better.

I encourage you, as you read these brief descriptions, to free-associate and build on them, adding your own meanings and associations. The irony of archetypes is that, while they are universal, they are also intensely personal and unique to us: if the archetype is the skeleton, the flesh and blood is your own. Think back to times in your life when you were living one of these archetypes out and fill in any blanks with your own lived experience. Try to consider them friends and guides.

THE INNOCENT

A childlike state in which you trust in powers greater than yourself, like Bambi before his mother dies. In shadow form, the

Innocent is gullible and passive, dependent, and reluctant to take chances and step into responsibility. If you're caught up in paralyzing fear and unwilling to go forth into the world, tempted to stay small and unseen, this is the Innocent in a wounded state. Conversely, the Innocent with boundaries, called on consciously, is conducive to wonderment and beginner's mind, both precious states of being.

THE ORPHAN

The child abandoned or neglected, seemingly alone in the world, forced to fend for itself, failed by institutions and family. Orphans can become cynical or dissociated by pain and find it easy to settle for less, born out of a belief that no one will ever come through for them. The upside of this archetype is becoming scrappy and finding your tribe—think Oliver Twist and his band of urchins or James and his insect friends flying through the clouds on a Giant Peach. I can't think of a single example of someone I know doing shadow work who hasn't been reintroduced to their Orphan, invited to remember its trials and soothe its pain. Integrating this archetype means loving and understanding the Orphan's wounds and anger and pledging to stand up for it in the present, while also respecting its toughness, even as it eventually softens as it learns to trust in your care.

THE WARRIOR

The passionate fighter venturing forth into the world to right wrongs, the Warrior is a disciplined protector of the weak. In its highest manifestation, it is strategic in fighting on behalf of the collective and sharing the spoils. Less enlightened versions lack integrity, indulge in sadism and power trips, and prey on the small to feel strong. It might pick fights with no chance of winning, disrespect opponents, or indulge in pointless violence. Warriors need righteous causes, and they need to be grounded, which isn't always easy when they taste power. It's your job to learn to harness that fighting spirit healthily and to know when to put it away.

THE CAREGIVER

The mother, the nurturing provider, the endless pool of empathy and love, the Caregiver often instinctually puts others first, which, when not bound by healthy boundaries, can lead to martyrdom and overdoing, a loss of centeredness. Caregivers who have been yoked to their role—women who became mothers against their will, for instance—can become resentful, distracted, and hurtful, the stereotype of the stressed-out, mean ER nurse but without the gallows humor. They can also live through others without tending to themselves. It's important to engage in self-care when you're in Caregiver mode, and to build space for separation as well as merging and service. One of the easiest ways to invoke the Caregiver, if you feel the lack of its soft, loving kindness in your life, is to adopt a pet, plant a garden, or volunteer for a mentoring role. If you're as big a fan of the TV series *The Wire* as I am, then you'll instantly think of the hit man Wee-Bey and how much he doted on his tropical fish.

THE EXPLORER

When you know there's an answer out there and you are driven to find it, you're hearing the Explorer's call. The Explorer often engenders solitude, a time when you're willing to make sacrifices of comfort and closeness with others to seek and find "out there." Young adults click into this archetype when they're looking for a career path or shaping their political identity or worldview.

Anyone on a psychedelic trip or a vision quest is tapping in. Sometimes the courageous spirit of the Explorer guides shadow work as you step carefully down into the dark. The downside of this energy is aimless wandering, an inability to anchor and commit, or using dilettantism as a distraction from other issues. Are you too often looking for something in the wrong places that you can never find? Or seeking surface validation in fleeting pleasures? Explorers transcend when they realize that the most meaningful discoveries are found within.

THE LOVER

The Lover is powered by the juiciest juice of life, the magic potion that attracts and revels in connection. It is the passion for living and the will to unite with another, free of mundane practicalities. Devoted, lustful, desirous of being known and adored, the Lover can also be codependent or addicted to sex and love without self-love, yearn for unattainable people, seduce indiscriminately, and lack common sense. The Lover enlightened holds space for the other and honors the self. The Lover is beautifully present during mirror work, when you gaze into your own eyes and hold yourself with profound, compassionate recognition.

THE CREATOR

Many ancient gods and goddesses who made the world were Creators. Creators translate inspiration into flesh and form. This is the archetype of the inventor, the artist, the scientist, and engineer. It's Iron Man and Madame C. J. Walker, the turn-of-the-century Black hair care entrepreneur and philanthropist. Outside any particular field, the Creator appears when you take your inner life seriously and work with inspirational tools to evolve something new into being, willing to use any and all appropriate means, especially if it's for the good of the collective. The shadow side of this archetype is creating negative self-fulfilling prophecies, taking on too much, or starting a million projects while bringing nothing to fruition.

THE DESTROYER

The bringer of death and calamity, the Destroyer tears the rug out from under us brutally. At the same time, phoenixlike, it creates space for the new, hopefully from a place of wisdom, surrender, and renewed gratitude for what has survived. Don't try to whitewash the devastation that comes with this archetype, who is a herald of disaster, plague, devastating accidents, sudden breakups, illnesses, and catastrophes. Respect its role in the natural order. Death is legitimately devastating but also a sacred passage. When repressed memories surface in shadow work, the Destroyer can be present, wiping away outworn ideas of who you are, or past-due strategies for comfort that kept you stuck. (With proper respect for the Destroyer, pledge to yourself that you will explore those memories gently and gradually.) The Destroyer demands that we give mourning and grief their rightful place. In its unhealthy guise, it can indicate an obsession with violence or sociopathy. A healthy perspective is being willing to end things definitively when need be.

THE RULER

The wise king or queen owns their power, takes responsibility for their actions, and leads by balancing duty with pleasure. The challenge is not to rest on your laurels or let past wins ossify into dogma—this is how kings and queens fall victim to their enemies. When the Ruler is operating successfully in your world, your systems are running smoothly, your people are provided for, your garden is weeded and seeded, and you feel steady at the helm. When it's gone awry, the result can be a petty tyrant, a zero-sum thinker, a control freak unable to trust in others, a skinflint, or a spendthrift.

THE MAGICIAN

The Magician governs the art of changing consciousness, of alchemizing suffering into higher meaning, of harnessing intuition, channeling, manifesting, visualization, active imagination, ritual, and divination. The healer or shaman feels their client's pain in their own body and helps transmute it. The therapist facilitates a breakthrough. Magicians understand chance and synchronicity, symbolism, and the importance of connecting to divine abundance. When out of whack, the Magician becomes an abusive guru or engages in toxic positivity, spiritual bypass (also a low manifestation of the Innocent), manipulation, or black magic.

THE SAGE

The elder who has learned the art of nonattachment, the Sage goes beyond subjective impression into universal truth, albeit with respect for human foibles and relativity. You step into your Sage when you have come out the other end of great trials, acquiring wisdom from lived experience, rather than gleaned from books or other secondhand sources. An unbalanced Sage is elitist, willfully obscure, dogmatic, all-knowing, addicted to perfection or cut off from all practical life. Cult leaders are out-of-bound sages, as is anyone who jealously hoards knowledge or healing tools from those who need them.

THE FOOL

Also known as the Jester or the Trickster, the Fool is the beginning of the journey, and the end. It bumbles into wisdom and has an uncanny knack for piercing truth—after all, only the Jester can speak pointedly to the king. The Fool is an ironic and deceptively complex figure—iconoclastic and untamable but sacred and ultimately serious, even if there is always divine humor in the air in its presence. The Fool often appears as a coyote in the indigenous cosmologies of the American Southwest. Or as Larry David crashing through privileged west LA in *Curb Your Enthusiasm*, his low-vibe antics revealing the hypocrisy and rigidity of his ostensibly more enlightened peers. In addition to upending the established order, the Fool governs the wide-eyed and unprepared energy of setting out onto a new path, as we all do to a certain extent in the face of the unknown. The Fool is present at the moment of death, as your soul passes through mystery to go on to its next home. Embarrassing mistakes are the Fool's territory, so don't beat yourself up over it when they happen. What can you learn from it, and how will you rebuild more solidly or gracefully after?

Making the effort to identify the archetypes presently at work in your life gives you the benefit of meaningful inspirational containers, and organizing forces, while you're getting in touch with old wounds and other shadow material. It encourages you to identify yourself as the protagonist in your life and see yourself as doing things for a sacred reason, no matter how unconscious, no matter how vexed or out of balance the results may feel at first. Once you identify an archetype active in you, how you live it out can show you whether you need to adjust your mission parameters.

At age seventy-seven, the astrologer Anne Whitaker models

the passage to both Sage and Fool. After losing her husband of thirty years, rather than isolate herself in her comfortable home, away from the turmoil of the outside world, as many women her age are expected to do, she moved her home office into a coworking space, where she is surrounded by much younger people. She had no idea what she was in for but has taken it as an opportunity to teach, listen, and learn. "The best way I can lead my life is to honor the life stage I'm at," she says, reflecting the detached wisdom of the Sage. "Getting older, in my opinion, is a process of gradually letting go of everything. Eventually you even have to let go of your life. Age can take just about everything away from you, your looks, your hair color, your loved ones, the strength of your bones. I feel quite countercultural, because women are encouraged not to claim their age. I hope it will inspire other people."

Whitaker is anything but your typical, prim "little old lady." She salts her conversation with swear words and sophisticated irony, surprising her young friends with her sense of adventure and sharp insight. Where she might have once felt out of place due to generational disconnect, she relishes the exchanges that put her in touch with cultural changes that she might not have understood on her own, softening other losses down the road that she knows will be hers to bear. In turn she's shown her office mates a dynamic way of aging, inviting them not to fear a necessary, inevitable, and potentially rewarding phase of life. Feeling the call of these archetypes and responding, Whitaker is not simply acted upon by the passing of time or the changing of circumstance.

Challenges become allies when we incorporate archetypal energy consciously and give each one its rightful place of honor. Importantly, this opportunity arises again and again in life, with every new important passage. We don't dance with our archetypes only once, we do it over and over, changing partners as we go.

"I had an amazing childhood in some ways," says Veronica, twenty-nine, from Austin, Texas, a former full-time tech worker turned consultant and content creator who embodied the Orphan and the Explorer for much of her young life. "I was traveling the world, but there was also a lot of domestic abuse. I'm Indian-Pakistani, so there is cultural and generational trauma, too. My father was very controlling and wanted to isolate my mother, so he moved us around all the time, to Australia, to Canada. I lacked a sense of belonging. As a third culture kid, I don't have a place where I'm from." By the time she was in high school, the trouble at home and her lack of a solid foundation put Veronica into a deep depression. She helped herself climb out slowly through yoga, therapy, meditation, journaling, and affirmations. Yoga and meditation, especially, became a constant solace, a place to return to for stability within, even if most of the time she still lived outwardly in limbo.

Veronica was able to imbue her Explorer with purpose. During high school, she volunteered abroad for the Amigos de las Américas, a kind of Peace Corps for teenagers, and more recently, she started a newsletter helping women like her find remote work, which has become her full-time meal ticket. But through it all, she never stopped moving. "It's kind of crazy how you repeat the chaos of your childhood. I've noticed in the past few years how I've reproduced it. I've been able to build a career, and it would be easy to say, 'No, my identity is traveling,' but I'm craving more stability now. I don't want to keep looking outside myself for answers, so I've become very focused on being true to myself. I'm trying to bring in more goddess energy." When I asked her to describe what the goddess meant to her, Veronica used words like "groundedness" and "earth energy." She is instinctively cleaving to an inspiring template—the figure of a solid, wise, and knowing sacred feminine—to help her nest and grow roots in a way she couldn't do before. As much as she changes her outer life to accommodate her heart's desire, she knows home is also inside her.

As Veronica continues to do shadow work, she has come to better understand her Orphan too, understanding how her father's neglect affected her relationship with her mother. Veronica leaning into her creative understanding of goddess energy is also a way of reclaiming a feminine role model that lifts her up and nourishes her, taking on the role of Caregiver to herself.

Lawrence, thirty-five, a massage therapist from Jacksonville, Florida, knew his Destroyer from an early age, but really owned his Caregiver only after he started shadow work. He grew up the privileged son of an opera singer and a military man. "I never had to worry about anything, but my mom and dad were always traveling," he recalls. When he was a young teenager, he and his siblings started acting out, "trying to call for attention." Inspired by an inner-city gangster movie, he got together with some friends and started doing home invasions. On one terrible night, one of his crew was shot in the head in front of him, and he was shot in the chest three times. In a moment, life as he knew it was over. He was only fourteen.

Lawrence spent four years in a juvenile detention facility, and near the end of his time there he interned at the Jacksonville medical examiner's office. He was promised a job upon release and spent the next fifteen years retrieving dead bodies, some from horrific crime scenes. "I got paid well for someone without a college degree, but it was a terrible job," he says. "Certain calls bothered me, like stuff with kids." Lawrence and his colleagues received training from the local FBI office to sequester their emotions. "They taught us to close off our personal feelings. Not to pray with the families of the victims, just show a straight face and collect the bodies." It helped him function professionally, but at great cost. He carried a lot of trauma and was eventually diagnosed with PTSD. After one particularly brutal work call in 2017, Lawrence drew the line and told his supervisors it was time for him to leave. Offered a year off and career retraining, "I went to the local community college and said, 'What's the opposite of the job I have now?' They told me, 'Massage therapist.'"

Lawrence discovered a talent for hands-on healing work, treating mostly athletes, but he was still trapped in overdoing to push away all the pain he hadn't processed. He cheated on his wife repeatedly, and, driven to remain a good provider, took on outside jobs, staying compulsively busy. Finally, he was forced to slow down when a case of the flu went haywire. The virus gave him vertigo for months and damaged his esophagus. "I couldn't breathe, I couldn't eat anything, I couldn't drive. It forced me to deal with myself." The Destroyer came calling once again.

Lying there all day alone in bed, Lawrence discovered shadow work online and, with literally nothing else to do, got started. "It was fill-in-the-blank exercises at first," he says, that made him aware of how much pain he was still holding on to. Then, responding to a journal prompt asking what he would see if he drew a picture of himself, "All I could see was black, just a black canvas. I saw myself as full of sadness." Another critical moment came doing mirror work. "I saw myself back when I was twelve," he recalls. "That was one of the years when my mom and dad were home a lot." In that moment, he viscerally connected to memories of feeling safe and taken care of, witnessing his parents having fun together as a loving couple. Reliving this again was healing.

Lawrence started going outside every day, something he never did before for pleasure, even though he had a large front lawn. He'd put his bare feet on the grass and soak up the sun, grounding and centering himself and feeling the warmth on his skin, sometimes for hours, if he had the time. "I started exploring joy," he says. "Before, if I had downtime, I was just knocked out."

As he learned to listen to his emotions in real time and focused on taking care of himself in basic and loving ways, he clicked into new habits naturally. “I started taking myself out to eat, spending more time with my wife and kids, just being in the moment. My boys never saw that inner child in me come out before,” he says. “Now if they want to do a water balloon fight, I do it with them.”

In therapy, nailing the wisdom of an archetype at a moment of crisis can usher in quantum leaps in healing. In a 2016 article for the journal *Thresholds*, the late John Rowan, once a fellow at the British Association for Counselling and Psychotherapy, wrote about one such instance that became a pivotal moment for one of his patients, where he used “the empty chair technique,” a way to externalize inner dialogue:

> Some years ago, a young man was in therapy with me and reported some very strange behavior. He was apparently undermining himself in a variety of ways, encountering problems with his training course, with his work, with his parents and with his girlfriend, all of which seemed to be self-inflicted. It suddenly occurred to me that perhaps this was the work of an archetype, perhaps the Trickster, perhaps Loki, perhaps the Devil [in the Tarot pack]. He agreed to explore this possibility using the empty chair technique, and we set up an extended session to explore this question. The result was an extraordinary explosion of emotion, which seemed to me to go well beyond the everyday limits of feeling, and to indeed represent something archetypal. As we went deeper and deeper into the material, I got the impression that sparks were flying off, so to speak, and that some real transformation was taking place. In the integration that followed, it seemed as though some bird had flown, and left behind a sense of peace and tranquility, which was quite different from anything that had gone before. The result was a complete change in the therapy, moving into

> an area which was much easier to handle than the extremes we had met before. There was now a deeper humanity which was both easier to work with, and undeniably more productive in the therapeutic effort.[3]

Other therapeutic modalities than classical Jungian analysis invoke archetypes in their own way. Internal Family Systems invites people to go deep inside to discover, comprehend, and soothe dissociated parts of themselves, all of which have their own personalities, identities, and roles. The adult you who is wise, caring, and curious is called the Self, like with Jung. Most parts are cleaved off from the Self as a protective mechanism, often in infancy and early childhood, but also later in life. "We each have a place in our psyche that determines our identity, choices, feelings and perceptions," writes the IFS educator Jay Earley, PhD, in *Self Therapy: A Step-by-Step Guide to Wholeness Using IFS*. "This seat can be occupied by Self or a part. Whomever resides in the seat of consciousness at any given moment is in charge of our psyche at that time."[4]

Parts protect each other, navigate life together, and often fight with each other, causing chaos and pain. They can have clear correspondences to Jung's better-known archetypes, each with a unique and subtle shading. In IFS, you might have ten different flavors of Orphan, several versions of Innocent, and some distinct kinds of Warrior, each with its own place and purpose and backstory. The goal of this work is to introduce the present you, grounded in your Self, to these parts, to get to know them consciously, with detailed awareness of their contours and functions, and develop trust so that you can hold space for them with respect, without being taken over.

Because the archetypes' domain is the unconscious, some of the most effective ways to contact them are through nonlinear means. There are many ways to do this intentionally. Two time honored, classic Jungian methods are active imagination and dream interpretation.

Active imagination is a self-guided visual meditation where you allow free association to reign supreme and follow where the inner images take you. It's a process where you become both the observer and the observed. In one session of active imagination, I found myself soaring high above vast, rolling valleys, a sense of exhilaration filling me as I glided effortlessly through the air. Below me, the landscape stretched out in a patchwork of greens and browns, the valleys giving way to a serene, glistening lake. As I flew, I noticed another bird beside me, its wings slicing through the air with graceful precision. I followed its movements closely, mimicking its turns and dives, learning to fly by embodying its fluid motions. Together, we swooped down, brushing past the tall grass and skimming just inches above the lake's shimmering surface. The cool spray from the water kissed my feathers as I flew, a tangible reminder of my connection to the world below.

Eventually, the bird disappeared, leaving me to fly solo. At first, I felt a pang of uncertainty, but then a newfound confidence surged within me. I navigated the skies alone, mastering the art of flight with every beat of my wings. This journey reflected my search for autonomy and freedom. I had always been dependent on others, seeking external input and validation to inform my direction. This experience taught me to lead myself and embrace the freedom within. It was a moment of encouragement from my unconscious, reminding me that while I had the gift of grounding and safety, I also needed to embrace my curiosity and freedom. In the thrill of the sky, I found the creativity and inspiration I had been lacking.

This process is no fairy tale, although the discoveries can be as enlightening as one as you learn which tales you tell yourself and others. Here is a step-by-step guide to try active imagination.

Active Imagination Exercise

1) Get calm and center yourself. Close your eyes and breathe deeply. Let everything else fall away as you allow an image or phrase or musical refrain to present itself to you—any symbol in any form. Don't worry, something always comes.

2) While remaining focused on what comes up, now fire up your imagination. Let the associations run wild, let that initial symbol twist and change and transform. Importantly, if what you're seeing is unpleasant or shocking, allow it to be. Do not judge what arises. It is information, not literal facts.

3) After a few minutes—you'll know when you're ready to stop—come back to present time. Now find a way to concretize what you envisioned. Drawing, collaging, or sculpting is the easiest way, because for many people, the act of writing might be too linear. The first time Jung dreamed his spirit guide Philemon, he painted his portrait. (You can look it up online on the website of the Philemon Foundation, philemonfoundation.org, a nonprofit working to prepare Jung's previously unpublished works for publication.) This doesn't have to be a masterpiece, it could be a doodle, although most of the time the image is too precious to dash off. Still, don't get hung up on perfection.

4) Now you have a talisman. Save it. Talk to it from time to time. If something about this symbol is out of bounds for you in your normal waking life, ask it why it does what it does and how it feels when it does it. You don't have to give a destructive archetype permission to run your life, but it came to you for a reason. Honor that and have an openhearted conversation with it.

There is a caveat with this practice. Jung engaged in a lot of active imagination at a delicate point in his life. He became so carried away with it, at one point he feared he had become psychotic. He credited being able to remember his training as a psychoanalyst for surviving the experience. This can be a powerful process, so don't overdo it or let it overwhelm you. Don't go on for hours. Maybe don't even do it every day, unless you are rock-solid grounded. I don't know a ton of people like that personally.

The other classic method of discerning archetypal energies or situations is through dream analysis. Dreams speak in symbols and puns; they use visual metaphors that are always invested with double and triple meanings from your own lexicon. While it can be tempting to rush to the internet for dream interpretation keys, don't take what you find there as gospel. Symbols and dream stories, while speaking in archetypes, are also open-ended and endlessly complex. Jung held that we come to a "correct" interpretation of a dream only by fluke. Hold your interpretations lightly as you let them guide you. You'll know if you're on the right track.

You don't usually need to go looking outside your own experience to analyze your dreams anyway. Last night, I dreamed that a basil plant that is currently thriving on my kitchen windowsill had shriveled and died. In the dream I was sad and disappointed, angry with myself and the plant over what happened. I woke up this morning asking myself what part of my life I was neglecting. I have been on a rigorous schedule lately. On the simplest level, this was a message from my unconscious to nurture myself. Perhaps also to cut up a tomato while they're still in season and have a snack. Perhaps also to set out some free time to dialogue with my Orphan, who still stings with the pain of earlier neglect, like that plant.

Dreams can get shocking when you're not paying attention to something important in your waking life. In another recent dream, I found myself at a school reunion, rekindling connections with friends from long ago. Suddenly, a man and a hooded figure appeared in the room and asked for something they were searching for—a key. I realized I had it and understood that the man and his accomplice were dangerous. They attacked the room, and I quickly jumped out of the window and started running, terrified of my Innocent being discovered by this Destroyer. I entered a tunnel that led to a home and dashed inside the master bedroom. As they closed in behind me, I hid in the closet, realizing I had nowhere to go.

Dreams can get shocking when you're not paying attention to something important in your waking life.

I woke up with my heart pounding, still feeling the fear in my body, and went to the window to look at the moon, which calmed me down. I have a few ideas on what that one was about, but I'm still not 100 percent clear on how to put together all those layers of imagery and meaning. This is why it's a great habit to write down your dreams. You can come back to them again and again until something clicks.

Dreams might also point to a future adventure or calling—your unconscious has ambitions for you too, and it knows where your true strengths lie, most of the time better than your ego does. If you're engaging in an alluring activity in a dream, or something that really charges or invigorates you, it may be a blinking light to dip into that activity in your waking life too.

No matter what, come at the symbols you find from all directions. Some Jungians take as a starting point the idea that each person appearing in a dream is an aspect of the dreamer themselves. In that light, my scary school killer is my own unacknowledged shadow Destroyer. I mentioned before that shadow work is a forever calling. I can start by asking where I am being too critical with myself, too violent with myself in self-recrimination. Where am I punishing myself for what I know? When can I give my Innocent the time to keep looking at the moon and know that she is safe?

Sometimes you encounter archetypes through synchronicity. This is another word we can thank Jung for. Essentially, it means meaningful random chance, or emotionally resonant symbols thrown into connection seemingly without cause. It is the foundational principle in divination systems like Tarot, Runes, and the *I Ching*, a collection of archetypes inscribed as hexagrams onto coins. All of them use a chance arrangement of symbols while posing a question—Runes and the *I Ching* are thrown, Tarot cards are shuffled and randomly picked out—to tell the inner story of the moment. Or is it so random? In an article on the C. G. Jung Institute of Chicago's *Junganthology* blog, Dennis Merritt, the analyst we met in Chapter Three, writes, "Synchronicity convinced Jung there was an element of the psyche outside of time and space: space and time are relative to the psyche."[5] Meaning, linear time and standard cause and effect do not govern the process of finding and making meaning.

Like Jung did with his patients later in life, Merritt incorporates the *I Ching* into sessions. Importantly, he doesn't do this seeking fixed outcomes or easy answers. "I spend an hour trying to discern what the issue is, and attempt to get to the most basic, appropriate question to put to the *I Ching*. Knowing what question to ask is an important part of the therapeutic process—it is half the battle as some say. If I feel the person wants to use the *I Ching* to short circuit a thoughtful, soul-searching wrestling with an issue, or has not gathered enough information, I discourage consulting [it]."

Dream Analysis Exercise

1) Write the dream down. Have a notebook next to your bed and do it the first thing when you wake up. Do not check your phone first. I repeat, do not check your phone first. Some people suggest writing the dream in the present tense to keep it as alive for you as possible in your conscious state. You may be groggy when you reach for your notebook, so do the best you can.

2) Give a thought to your present life conflicts once you've gotten the dream down on paper. What's pressuring you? What's scaring you? What are you avoiding? What might this dream be trying to rectify for you or compensate for?

3) Take an extra moment with the most central figures. Is there a victim or a predator? A hero or a villain? Is the main character even human, or something like a giant clock or a ship or a bird? Grab your notebook and write down whatever comes to mind around each one of these especially grabby symbols or dynamics. Your unconscious has access to all these associations. It knows the territory. Take some time to get to know it yourself.

4) Like with active imagination, if you're really fascinated by something in one of your dreams or haven't yet grasped it to your satisfaction, draw it, paint it, write a poem about it, or do something else creative in tribute. You can then keep the conversation going, like with active imagination. Creative acts are gas in the unconscious's tank. Plunging into a dream symbol in this way tells your unconscious that the door is open, and you're eager to know more.

Madeline Bolin, a Tarot reader based in Austin, Texas, maintains the same spirit in readings with her clients. She is relatively new to the practice, having picked it up for self-study during a dark night of her soul during Covid confinement.

The Tarot first emerged in the fifteenth century in Europe, as playing cards. Traditionally, it's comprised of numbered suits representing the four elements, culminating in Pages, Knights, Queens, and Kings, and a series called the Major Arcana, twenty-one important archetypes unto themselves. Our friend the Fool is the first, at number zero, and the numbers rise as the archetypes pass through a sequence that symbolizes the soul's journey. They include representations of catastrophe, judgment, rulership, inspiration, intuition, compulsion, death, and they culminate in the World—the celebration of true integration here and now on earth.

"I remember being given my first Tarot deck during confinement," Bolin says. "I faced a lot of my shadows then. I locked myself in a three-hundred-square-foot house, just myself and my cards, and was able to meditate with them. I stared at each one for an hour and asked myself, 'Why did I just pull this card? What does that red dot in the image mean? Why does it have a salamander?' In that dark time, I would say to myself, 'I know I drew this card today so I could focus on its teachings.' Sometimes it was insightful, like the Strength card, sometimes it was like the Six of Pentacles, which means you've just got to keep working. It allowed me to be present and not get overwhelmed with where I was going to be in three months or six months or a year."

Bolin got so intimately connected with her cards that she started a side business doing readings for others. "I like to say that I have two lives," she says. "I have my magical life and my muggle life. My muggle side is my corporate job, in which I get to exercise a lot of my competitive energy and be disciplined and rooted in this world, which I think serves me well at this time in my life. The magical side has really inspired me."

While people often contact readers of all kinds in a panic state, feeling lost and desperate to find themselves, or when they're desirous of a companion and insecure about it—in other words, when they're in the grip of some kind of inner archetypal struggle—"I tell people, like anything in life, don't go into it with expectations," Bolin says. "You're going to explore, with very clear intentions. If you're just spewing an outcome that you want, like is this boy going to text me back, the cards will quickly put you in your place. I like to tell clients that Tarot is about the soul's journey. We're all going to experience magic, love, strength, luck, death. Right now, in your soul's journey, you might not get what you came to ask the cards about."

Sometimes clients come scared about a possible outcome before the reading starts. For Bolin, "that means your intention is telling you there's a darkness within you, or a dark situation around you that needs to be expressed. And if you're afraid of that darkness coming to light, you might not be ready to hear it. So maybe we should reschedule. However, if you're able to understand that with darkness comes light, let's see what that dark card is if it comes up. Let's say it's the Tower, about upheaval and change and being swept off your feet in an uncomfortable way. Know that the next card in the Major Arcana is the Star, signified by a woman dipping her hands into the water on her way to enlightenment, relishing the beauty. If you're able to look the Tower in the eye, you can then say, okay, let's get through this, let's get to the inspiration of the Star." With any kind of divination, the key is to be open to the moment and not rush to finish the story.

It's also tempting when diving into eternal, powerful symbols and archetypes to get a little carried away with the ego, thinking you've unlocked the secrets of the universe. Jung called this inflation, when you overidentify with a particular figure—perhaps the Magician? He saw it as a regression, not a stable or healthy place to be. None of us are meant to bury ourselves in our unconscious. We're meant to dip in, to exchange, to listen, and then to return to waking life more curious, open, resilient, and self-forgiving. As we sift through the sediment of our psyche, identifying the micro elements that construct our macro whole—our actions, emotions, and archetypal influences—we begin to map out the landscape of our inner world.

Engaging with archetypes is not only done on the surface. This work, like shadow work, is a process of alchemy—a radical reimagining of ourselves and our relationship to the world. Long before the Enlightenment, alchemy was a magical practice. It was both a literal search for missing ingredients to turn lead into gold and a metaphor for the human effort to reach the divine in the here and now.

In the spirit of alchemy, it's only by understanding and integrating universal archetypes, as sources of inspiration and healing, that we can transcend our fragmented selves. Instead of letting archetypes control you, through contemplation and shadow work allow them to empower you. Choose your next archetype consciously, listening carefully for its call, as you envision a more authentic version of yourself at whichever grand stage in your life you are. Surround yourself with the symbols and objects that will infuse this chosen archetype into your space and your internal world. Whether it's a poster of the Beatles on the wall to inspire your Creator or a piece of nature to embody the Sage, let these worldly reminders of a deeper truth guide and support your journey toward wholeness.

FIVE

THE SHADOW IN INTIMACY

Knowing your own darkness is the best method for dealing with the darknesses of other people.

—C. G. JUNG, IN A 1937 LETTER TO KENDIG B. CULLY[I]

It's hard to think of an area of life as ripe for shadow work as intimate relationships—both in the ways we seek partnerships and in the kinds of connections and projections we live together once we establish them. People need love. They need to be seen at their tenderest, to be adored and desired. There may be more pages, poems, stories, and movies that try to soothe this grand human longing than just about any other subject matter on earth. Jung understood the pull of romantic love well, and saw it, like so many other challenging, compelling, archetypal passages of life, as a road back to greater self-understanding and wholeness. We are so vulnerable in the presence of a lover when we stand, often literally, naked. Unfortunately, this so often leads us to try to flatter, cajole, and seduce rather than show up fully and honestly, with faith that we can be loved for who we are.

Given the sensitive, fully loaded, shadowy beings we all are by the time we start to feel romantic longing, the question is naturally complicated. There's the first spark of attraction, itself a subject dense with signification. There's the building trust and mutual care with a potential partner, when you show yourself, warts and all, to one whose esteem you yearn for and on whose presence you come to count. This too, is far easier said than done.

Shadow work is an essential for this field of our lives. If we're single and looking or already coupled, it helps us get a handle on the kind of lover we can truly be. It puts partnership, if you're in one, into a higher state of functioning, like it has for me. It will help you know more clearly if you need to leave an unworkable situation and help you find your way to more aligned potential mates if you're looking. It will empower you to take time out to work on yourself alone, if that's what you need, knowing you'll come back another day, fuller, more present, more available, and more discerning.

No matter what level of maturity you have reached or what life experience you already have, building a loving, intimate relationship with another person—one of the greatest blessings there is in life—is never a simple or automatic prospect. Indeed, we make better choices in love if we've done shadow work, and we have more fulfilling, resilient, and solid relationships if we keep doing it, either openly with our partners, or each of us on our own.

This chapter will look at how shadow work can prepare you for love by helping you get to the root of issues of worth, attractiveness, and trust so you can figure in another person's life more serenely, with more of who you are. We'll talk about the shadow pitfalls around dating and pinpoint important questions everyone should ask. We'll also look at the delicate passage into partnership, when the mask tumbles and you start to find out who the other really is and who you can become together. And lastly, we'll investigate how the shadow persists in couples and how to mine it for its extraordinary potential, both individually and together. We'll unpack some useful techniques for navigating love in the most conscious way possible, showing what shadow work for couples can look like either when it's undertaken with your partner or when it's done by just one person, in service of the health of the whole. Both are a kind of balm for healthy connection.

In the embrace of another,
we meet ourselves anew.
The dance of love is the dance with our shadows,
an invitation to grow,
to heal,
to become whole.
It's not about perfection,
but about seeing each other clearly,
in the light and in the dark,
and choosing to stay,
to love,
to transform.
You and me,

They and we,
are more connected,
Than it may seem.

You see:
Love is everyone's dominant gene,
Love is in everyone's family tree,

Love is the breath of humanity,
Love is the stillness beyond the world's entropy.

I know many people who came to *The Shadow Work Journal* out of frustration and pain in their search for love—from wanting to stop compulsive romantic patterns to finally find a healthier connection, to experiencing love without abuse, to healing after a heartbreaking split so they can put themselves out there again wiser and more evolved. Like any other kind of suffering, pain in love is your shadow pointing the way to you becoming fuller and more authentic by looking with forgiveness and appreciation at who you are and have been in relationships. Remember that like every other passage in life, through love, even painful love, we are playing out an unconscious soul drive to seek healing and integration. Know that this pain, despite your best efforts, isn't a sign of your unfixable defectiveness or of being unlovable or unsuited for coupling.

The whole question might be less fraught if our culture didn't invest so heavily in the idea of living happily ever after with one special perfect person—an escapist, immature fantasy fed to us since we were little, with immense power to distort expectations. The notion that someone out there can simply complete us and make it all better is so alluring that too often we persist as Innocents and Fools, yearning for someone else to show up and magically heal it all for us. Jung was clear that the temptation to project shadow stuff onto another is one of the biggest challenges to grappling with it in yourself. We too often use the fantasy of perfect romantic love to ignore our own inner wounds instead of confronting them. Which is ironic, because we'd be so much better off in real, authentic, honest love than an illusion anyway.

We're inundated with toxic cultural stereotypes worth rooting out as you consider the role of love in your own life, and your expectations and assumptions about it. These misconceptions are deeply embedded in our collective psyche, and you'll undoubtedly recognize many of them:

1. OBSESSION IS LOVE

In movies, all-consuming infatuation looks romantic and exciting, but in real life it's not sustainable. True connection requires a stable foundation. Prioritizing intense emotions over shared, mundane, soft experiences is misleading and can open the door to gaslighting and abuse.

2. IT'S ALL ABOUT THE RING

Relationships are messy and imperfect. The true purpose of partnership is navigating these flaws together. Commitment demands daily effort, communication, and compromise. Marriage isn't the end; it's the beginning of the real journey.

3. I MUST FIND MY SOULMATE/TWIN FLAME

Believing in a single perfect match sets unrealistic expectations and can keep you stuck in a situation that has turned toxic. Soulmates are simply people who help your soul move forward on its path. They come in many forms: friends, family, even adversaries. We encounter many throughout our lives, not just one, and they aren't always with us until the end.

4. IT'S UP TO ME TO HELP MY PARTNER CHANGE

While relationships foster growth, it's not your job to change your partner's core being. Their path is theirs to walk, and you're there to support, not to steer.

5. LOVE CONQUERS ALL

The notion that love alone can overcome everything ignores the need for trust, respect, communication, and shared goals. Love by itself isn't enough to conquer addiction or abuse. That takes time, commitment, and often outside help. Love, regard, adoration, respect: these are all the gas in the tank, but they're not the whole car.

6. UNDYING PASSION, AND CONSTANT SEX, ARE THE NORM

In long-term relationships, desire ebbs and flows. Quiet moments of affection that don't lead to sex are as important as those thrilling moments of passion.

7. FIGHTING IS UNHEALTHY

Conflicts are natural and essential for growth. Healthy disagreements lead to progress. Here I am not talking about repetitive, unresolved fights, or conflict turning to violence or abuse.

When you're single and setting out to find a mate is another time when the excavation of shadow work, revealing to you the areas where you feel weak, small, or unworthy—and, importantly, how and why it all came to be—is immensely empowering. Knowing the trigger points in your self-esteem forearms you when you meet potential prospects, when it so often feels like you have more riding on approval than, say, in a platonic friendship. And it shows you where you need to heal. It's often said, and it's true: it's hard for someone else to love something in you that you don't love in yourself.

"When I have clients coming to me saying, 'I want a boyfriend, I want a girlfriend, I want a partner,' I'm like, 'Great, know what you want,'" says Madeline Bolin, the Tarot reader we met in the previous chapter. "That's step one. Now be it yourself. Be your own partner. The Lovers card, while it's so beautiful, is all about being a mirror. If you're not attracting the partner that you want in life, it's because you're not ready to face yourself in the mirror, or when you look into it, you're not seeing something you want to see."

Appropriately, mirror work is the perfect technique to address this. A long, extended communion with your own reflection—and the soul that lives inside it—is an exercise in respectful intimacy. More than that. The eyes are a universe unto themselves, a portal that bridges the conscious and unconscious realms. The pupil, a black hole that pulls you in, is surrounded by the swirling patterns of the iris, as detailed and complex as the galaxies we marvel at in the night sky.

When you sit before a mirror, you're not just reflecting light, you're front and center before the reflection of your life itself. In mirror gazing, you encounter the infinite within you. It's a sacred moment, a communion with the self, where you're both the observer and the observed, the traveler and the vast landscape within. In those moments, the eyes reveal what lies beyond the surface, like a glimpse of the mysteries, the conscious and the unconscious revelations we hold inside.

Mirror work invites you to confront your beliefs about yourself with tenderness. It's an act of radical self-acceptance, where you stand face-to-face with your own humanity and see what you've turned away from, neglected, or rejected: not just the wrinkles of time, but the scars of past wounds, the vulnerabilities that make you human. This practice is more than just self-reflection; it's self-relation. You begin to see the connection between how you relate to yourself and how you'll relate to others. If you cannot offer compassion to the person in the mirror, how can you offer it to a partner?

In preparing for romantic love, mirror work is foundational. It's a way to soften the edges of your self-criticism and build a relationship with yourself that is rooted in kindness and understanding, not in judgment. This becomes the blueprint for how you will engage with another.

When you can look in the mirror and witness yourself loving yourself as you are, you prepare yourself to receive and give love

Mirror Work Exercise for Greater Self-Love

1) Sit in front of your reflection. Breathe deeply as you adjust from that first surface glimpse of your face and lock into your own eyes.

2) Continue to breathe as you take a good, solid minute to commune with your soul. Feel the goodness reaching out from inside you. Feel the fullness of the heart that is beating.

3) Now ask yourself, "What parts of me do I find hard to love?" Take a minute, without breaking your gaze, to see what surfaces.

4) Speak the answers to yourself as if you were speaking to another person, including why you think these "hard to love" parts came to be. The highest, wisest, and holiest part of you is listening. Pour out your heart.

5) If it helps you come to clarity, you can also take out your journal and recap your conversation. Include how the experience made you feel.

6) If you took a journaling break, now come back to the mirror and reset your gaze. Repeat the following phrase: "I am whole and complete, and I love myself for all of who I am. I love every vulnerability. I love every flaw. I love every strength."

in its truest form—unconditional, unafraid, and unencumbered by the shadows that once kept you from seeing your true self. In this light, the mirror becomes more than a tool; it becomes a portal. A doorway to deeper self-awareness, self-compassion, and, ultimately, the capacity to love another with the same grace and acceptance you've learned to extend to yourself.

Indeed, the truest kind of self-love means committing to building loving shadow awareness. All shadow work, whether in front of the mirror or elsewhere, is a vow to yourself, a deep "I do," even when you're flailing and miserable, when you're sick, weak, and feeling without options, just as much as when you're on top of the world.

PREPARING FOR LOVE

Shadow work certainly helps lay bare our true motivations in seeking a mate. So we often strive to right the wrongs of our past. We look for nurturing where we once felt neglected, admiration where we were disdained. We seek support where we were undermined and want to feel proud of our goodness instead of feeling shame. We yearn to be recognized and validated, for our hearts to beat faster, to be enveloped in the other, to trust and be trusted, to share without fear. These are noble desires, and they are possible to achieve—but only if the shadow isn't unconsciously running the show.

When that's happening, what should be a choice is often a compulsion, an addiction to a destructive type or to an abusive pattern that replicates suffering. The shadow creeps into love in small and large ways: in overreacting to minor sins, an ongoing need for validation from your partner, difficulty trusting them, sabotaging intimacy by avoiding it, and so much more.

If we haven't taken the time to confront and work with our shadow, we often end up reliving the pains we tried to escape. The wounds we refuse to acknowledge remain in control, and in their unconscious state, they strive to repeat the original injury over and over because it's the only thing that seems real. Most of the time, it stems from what we grew up experiencing as normal.

As a woman, the girl whose father ignored her might choose men who do the same, even if it breaks her heart over and over. The adult who was never held by their mother wonders why they have a hard time being touched. When the boy who was forced to reject his own sensitivity becomes a man, he might look for it in partners who don't know that they're signing up to be primary emotional laborers, when all they really are is another human being as messy and tortured as he is.

If we haven't taken the time to confront and work with our shadow, we often end up reliving the pains we tried to escape.

"If someone is constantly attracted to unavailable people, what's going on?" asks Connie Zweig in a conversation we had on the August 4, 2024, episode of my *Zenfulnote* podcast. "What is the shadow trying to achieve? I would say it's trying to wake us up to an old pattern of an unavailable parent. 'Well, my dad never comes home from work, but he loves me.' Love equals Daddy's at work, so then the shadow draws us into that dynamic in order to make it conscious."

Zweig sees dating consciously as its own kind of shadow work. "The shadow is guiding us in our attractions to other people," she continues. "We're unconsciously drawn to people and feel a kind of attraction or aversion to them because of the shadow. Because of the early messages that we carry in the unconscious, about what's attractive, what's appropriate, what's successful, what's generous."

The shadow is always there behind our perfectly made-up faces and coiffed hair anyway. "Often when we're dating, we're kind of in a persona, we want to look our best and be on our best behavior," Zweig continues. "And that doesn't really let people in, it doesn't allow them to really get to know us. And the other person is doing the same thing." She suggests paying close attention to all these encounters as opportunities to root out your shadow characters behind the mask. "You meet different people, and you begin to see what arises in you when you're with them." What needy part of your inner child is hiding in plain sight this time? The people pleaser? The little girl or boy who would walk over cut glass to get Mommy to smile? The one who learned to hold themselves aloof and let others come to them to feel powerful? That little you is there on your date, every bit as important as the person you're sitting across the table from.

Lee Oren, LCSW, a therapist I connected with based in Waterford, Connecticut, also advises asking yourself questions to get to the root of what is really happening during a first date while it's going on—questions that center how you honestly feel in the moment: "Do I like what they're asking me about myself when we first meet? Do I like how I feel in my body when I'm with them? Does the silence feel okay when the conversation stops flowing? Am I dissociated somewhere else, analyzing our interaction, or am I allowing myself to feel what's happening in the moment? Am I naturally, spontaneously smiling? These are all things that are hopefully happening automatically and authentically when you're just being yourself with another person you're interested in."

If there's any discomfort or stress in the other's presence, identify it and let it speak to you, either to yourself in the moment, or in contemplation later. Zweig recalls, "One woman I interviewed for [her book] *Romancing the Shadow: A Guide to Soul Work for a Vital, Authentic Life*, said to me, 'I knew in my body he was dangerous, but I didn't pay attention.' Some people have an inner dialogue—'There's something off here, I think he's lying'—but they don't always listen to what it's saying." The desperation to find someone great may speak louder than the truth of the interaction.

For some people who have experienced abuse, without shadow work, a loving connection to another might not even be possible. I don't want to imply that we are living our highest lives only if we're in a committed couple. Singleness is also a valid choice, as is polyamory—which Alfred, whom we met in Chapter Two, discovered for himself too. "When people talked about, Oh, yeah, you've got to find your other half, I didn't like how that sounded, like I'm incomplete," he says. "That snowballed for me more as I started doing shadow work."

But many people who hold themselves apart from intimacy due to a history of trauma and dissociation still yearn for deep connection and struggle to get past shadow fears of being seen, and the learned experience of being abused, to make themselves available to it. Once again, the primary work comes in opening up first to themselves, and saying "I do."

Oren describes one of her patients, a woman now in her late twenties, who started therapy with her seven years ago, and for whom an extended course of shadow work yielded extraordinary results. "She came in initially for help with anxious physical symptoms, harming herself, poor eating habits, impulsivity, and no long-term romantic relationship experience," Oren recalls. "She had a history of sexual trauma that was not revealed for several years but turned out to be the basis for the shadow work she needed to explore. She would let her body be used, saying, 'I'm in control of it. I'm the one who tells them they can't stay over,' but in other ways her boundaries weren't strong enough. Then she would be really down on herself and often would just withdraw."

It took Oren and her patient several years of working with stream-of-consciousness writing, journaling, dream analysis, and talk therapy before the woman could face the guilt and shame that came from being a victim of abuse and understand that it wasn't her fault. This was the kernel of why she hurt herself and held herself so apart from everyone else, and from love. Oren's patient knew that her patterns with men were unhealthy, but she was powerless to change them until she got to the root of her abuse, and of who she was as a soul beyond it.

In sessions where Oren would have her patient close her eyes and simply let memories come, in the safe space of her office, the awareness of her patient's history of suffering came through her body first. "I'd ask her to be blank and see what comes in, and at first she just said she felt numb." Then she'd have flashes, with memories of her abuse triggered through things like smells. Little by little, she allowed herself to feel the emotions that she had so long ago tried to sever from her conscious life, and she was able to integrate the pain she had hidden from herself, and everyone else too. "Writing in her journal was her freedom," Oren says. "And being able to experience her pain in a safe setting was absolute freedom."

Soon she softened the hypervigilance she had developed, eventually creating a truly loving relationship with herself, where she more instinctively pays attention to her own needs and honors them. "She found who she was again by understanding the dark past that haunted her for years," Oren says, "and working through the hurt, pain, unconscious pull it kept having. Her inner child was taken care of and safe in the therapeutic process, and she came to trust her inner voice as a young adult and set up her life to cater to it."

It was that newly developed muscle of self-care that made Oren's patient change to a lower-pressure job leaning into caregiving herself. And then, after truly becoming a partner to herself, setting her own boundaries and learning to recognize her inner voice when it spoke, she met a guy who turned out to be caring and sensitive himself. "Because she had gotten so in touch with herself," Oren says, "she could sense this was a healthy person, on the same intelligence level, and in touch with himself, too." They're now in a committed relationship, the first she has ever had.

The conscious search for the beloved demands that we put everything we care about on the table. It asks us to know what we need and want for our future, to be clear on how we spend our time, and to consider how much space we can create for another in our lives. That's already a formidable task. Shadow work can be our greatest tool here, because it strips away the illusions of who we are, acting as a tuning fork to help us better refine the kind of person and energy we want to be, and be with.

The conscious search for the beloved demands that we put everything we care about on the table.

The unconscious wants what it wants. In doing shadow work, some people get in touch with desires that are far from what society or even they themselves consider "normal." Active imagination can kick up some unusual stuff. So can dreams. So can daily life. If you start digging around in new parts of your consciousness, you may find some new desires. You might discover some of them are unconventional. This, too, is an up-leveling, in that it is a truly honest reckoning. In the spirit of shadow work, embrace what you find.

For example, kinks do not have to be pathologies, they do not have to be harmful to others or self-debasing when they arise from deep inside us. It's okay to explore them with others, as long as you're clear on ethical lines and not in a situation of abuse or coercion. This is all part of defining the kind of lover you truly are and the kind of lover you truly want to seek.

Mistress Damiana Chi, PhD, runs the Evolutionary Dominatrix Academy in Los Angeles and has over two decades of experience helping people play out their need for submission, whether as a kink-informed life coach, trainer of professional dominatrices, or as a dominatrix herself. She works as a sexual soul healer, steering submissive clients and future dommes through what could feel like a chaotic and dangerous space. "The BDSM motto is 'safe, sane, and consensual,' but I want to add 'ethical' to that too," she says. She mentions internet relationships where submissives will be charged high rates just to speak to dommes, or relationships of brutality and exploitation that include permanent marking, and mind games that persist beyond the boundaries of sessions, treating the other not as a playmate who might enjoy messing around with consensual humiliation for a time, but as real prey with no limits. It can be hard to see the lines in the throes of a new thrill, which is why ethical partners are so important here.

"For me the first step of the process was confronting my darkest desires and taking the first step to making them real by actually talking about them," writes Chi's client "J," who came to see her with no previous experience in BDSM. "As we spoke openly, I could feel the deepest part of my soul exhaling for the first time. . . . I experienced a great deal of mental relief letting go of suppressed feelings that had been kept inside for so long." Another client, "Bruce," says, "To be truly 'seen' for the first time in my life, and to be fully accepted, lifted decades of guilt and shame from my soul, the heaviness of which I cannot put into words."

"I'm disintegrating the power of shame that they've carried around with them for years," Chi says. "Shame is an illusion that holds people back from being their full authentic selves, loving themselves fully for who they are." None of Chi's clients would have been able to live out these moments of true liberation if they hadn't first admitted to themselves what they really wanted and loved themselves enough to find the right partner with whom to step out and explore.

STAYING HEALTHY IN LOVE

Let's say you're one of the lucky ones and a good date turns to two, three, and more. Zweig says now is the time to put the big stuff on the table, to ask yourself, and your intended other, the important questions. "What do you believe, and what are your values? What do you want in your life? What is your life purpose? How are you going about that?" Zweig says to watch your own response and watch the other's in as clear-eyed a fashion as possible. "Let's say it's a woman who is [having this conversation] with a man. And the man says, 'I only care about making money. I want to feel financially secure and that's my priority.' What comes up for her? How does that align with her vision of her life inside? Her values, her meaning? If that's not compatible from the get-go, do you think that there is still a chance for a healthy relationship to be formed?" People can be different and still form great connections. But they need to know what their red flags are—they always point to the shadow. Prospective partners need to ask themselves, "What are the nonnegotiables for me?" Zweig says. "Be really clear about it." And if you start to see a red flag waving, "Don't rationalize it. 'I can change him. He'll stop doing that. She'll be different if I love her.'" All that is the shadow talking.

The urge to seek connection with another is deeply rooted in us, and it's not inherently codependent or negative. But even when we enter relationships from a place of wholeness, we shouldn't expect the other person, or the relationship itself, to provide enduring peace. (Nor should we view the success or failure of these unions as a measure of our own worth.) There is always a bumpy adjustment when the shadow comes out to play.

There is always a bumpy adjustment when the shadow comes out to play.

I grew up closed off and shy. I was a secret, hopeless romantic and sheltered, especially, by my older brother, who was my biggest supporter and protector. None of my ideas of love were rooted in reality, but they glimmered in the waves of my imagination while I waited for something profound to come find me.

I remember sitting in my college dorm room in my first year, my feet hanging over my bed, gazing out of the window. I didn't have my brother there to shield me anymore, but I had been dedicating hours every day to prayer and meditation, and I joined a church choir. I knew I was ready to step into the open gates of love. Out of the blue, almost, I felt ready to meet someone for real. I affirmed it out loud, and I wrote it in my journal: I was calling my future husband and sent him love, whoever he would turn out to be.

Abe found me through my singing during an impromptu musical jam session with a mutual friend. I had no idea my voice would draw him in, but isn't that the epitome of romance? I wasn't thinking about the letter I had written weeks before. I wasn't searching. I wasn't trying to look cute for him. I was just expressing myself and being myself, and by doing that, he saw me as I really was.

Our friend thought we were too different: I was too "pure" and churchy, and he was too bombastic and sharp. And we were, and are, different, but I've learned that sometimes, the greater the contrast in personalities, the rarer and more beautiful the colors that come from the sparks of connection. Logic can take you from A to Z and 1 to 100, but love catapults you beyond reason into the realm of the uncontainable, unconditional, and indescribable.

When we met, it wasn't too long before I went on the self-healing research mission that led me to shadow work. It ended up being a critical tool for helping the two of us blend better, because I could step back and analyze the differences in our temperaments that once before might have felt threatening. In helping me mature, shadow work also helped Abe and me create what we call "our bubble"—that little love island that only the two of us inhabit. It's our shorthand, our shared language, our shared space. It's what Zweig, in her book *Romancing the Shadow*, calls the third body, an alchemical miracle greater than the sum of its parts. The third body is like a field generated by the relationship that's bigger than each individual member of the unit.[2] It's not the couple's persona or how it relates to the outside world. It transcends their individual identities, merging the essence of both partners into something greater. Ideally, it's a sacred space where true connection and mutual growth occur, a joint presence that evolves and flourishes through shared experiences. In nurturing this third body, we tap into a deeper well of wisdom, compassion, and unity, enriching our journey together.

In *Romancing the Shadow*, Zweig explains that the third body can't be born until a relationship is truly established—until each person has uprooted the weeds in the couple's common garden and planted and tended it together, through frost and drought, until some illusions have shattered. Once third bodies are formed, it's still up to each person to keep them fed and watered and inspired throughout their time on earth. An ongoing commitment to shadow work, alone and together, is a relationship's greatest ally.

"Everything that irritates us about others can lead us to an understanding of ourselves," Jung wrote.[3] Maturity is essential for a relationship of any kind to work, but many adults are stuck in their child's mind, acting out. The good news and the bad news are the same: because nothing pushes our buttons like intimate partnership and its lived experience, exploring this type of love is one of the most concentrated, extra-strength opportunities for personal development that we have as humans. Sexy vacations and date nights aren't the point. Growth is, whether you stay together forever or you don't.

The shadow helps us form the third body. "Committed partnerships are ecosystems that are designed to force both people up against themselves and each other, over and over, day after day," writes the trauma therapist Resmaa Menakem, MSW, LICSW, SEP, in *Monsters in Love: Why Your Partner Sometimes Drives You Crazy—and What You Can Do About It*. "Both partners get ground together in the same way that a rock gets polished into a jewel. Over and over, you and your partner have a choice: you can polish each other into jewels or you can grind each other into dust."[4]

"The conflicts you have with your mate aren't just about differing backgrounds or needs or communication styles or approaches to life," he writes. "*They are about each of you becoming the person you want to be (or, at least, ought to want to be).* That's the opportunity of the relationship."[5]

"While we're dating and keep choosing the same people, it's the shadow that's leading us around," says Zweig. "Then we marry the person and think we know them. But we only know them on their best behavior in the romantic cycle, and then what happens? The shadow starts to erupt, and we're shocked. 'What? You drink alcohol every night?' 'What? You're going to criticize me like that when you're hurt?' This is one of the reasons for the high rate of divorce, because when they meet either their own shadows or their partner's shadows, most people don't have tools to work it through and get to what I call a shadow marriage." That shadow marriage is the ultimate goal, but you have to understand what the dynamics are first.

Here are a few typical examples to show you what I mean:

1) Partner A is a bootstrapping self-made warrior who grew up thinking that asking for help was a sign of weakness. Now A believes they should shoulder every big responsibility in the couple, from providing to deciding. Partner B loved feeling taken care of at first, which clicked in so well with their own childhood experience of not being capable or strong enough to handle anything. This dynamic settled into a pattern of A overdoing, then feeling overwhelmed and taken advantage of, and B feeling unimportant and without any say in their shared lives. Resentment brewed and turned into fights filled with blame and turning away from each other.

2) Partner A and B are deeply in love. A grew up with strict discipline, with firm boundaries and consequences, and believes that's the right way to go. B had a more open and freewheeling upbringing, where emotions were given free expression and creativity was prized. It was only when B got a positive pregnancy test that this difference turned into a conflict. Faced with a terrifying change (and thrilling blessing), each started to worry whether the other was up to the task. Now the child comes, and these differing approaches and eroding trust become inflexible ideologies, each seeking to invalidate the other, with poor baby C now the battlefield of their tensions.

3) A and B seem to have been together for years and seem to be the perfect couple, but beneath the apparent harmony, there's a subtle dance of manipulation that neither fully acknowledges. They know where all the fears, insecurities, and soft spots in the

other lie, and they use it against each other in a passive-aggressive battle neither is courageous enough to call out. A, aware of B's deep fear of abandonment, withholds affection or attention during disagreements and uses silence as a tool to gain control. B, knowing A's insecurity around financial stability, overspends and subtly suggest that A's contributions aren't enough, planting seeds of doubt that tilt the balance of power in their favor. All this is woven into their verbal and nonverbal communication. Look closely enough and you see that the overt warmth is phony, an investment they have in how they come across to everyone else.

4) A is affectionate and giving, and then when his buttons are pushed one time too many, he explodes into a snarling rage beast, going from zero to sixty in a breath. A's family always fought loud and hard and made up in the end. But B comes from a family where emotional control was prized, and every utterance was given careful thought. A's rages seem like innocent eruptions of feeling to A. To B they are terrifying, causing her to shut down little by little until she walks on eggshells to avoid the storm. They stop having sex entirely and have started to ignore and avoid each other.

In all these cases, it's not about who's at fault, but about becoming aware of the patterns that keep them stuck. The first step is to recognize the dynamics. The next step is to hash it all out without starting a fight about it, reinforcing closeness and investing in the third body rather than more distance and blame.

What if, instead of pointing fingers, A and B looked at the shadow dynamics in their couples as characters of their own? What if they saw the poison they've started to ingest regularly as its own personality—like the shadow of their third body, if you will? They can name this shadow dynamic and treat it as a misunderstood friend to be heard and forgiven. "Our kid fight," "Our control game," "Our bitchy nitpicker." This takes personal blame out of the equation and helps them shoulder the burden of the conflict together. It makes it easier to ask each other what's really going on, what the pattern gives each one, and what it takes away. In seeing the relationship's shadow not as a personal flaw but a shared challenge, there is room for more harmonious transformation.

Respect becomes the alchemy of this process. It's about making space for each other's full selves—flaws, shadows, and all—without pathologizing or sternly correcting. Respect isn't solely about listening; it's about truly witnessing each other, recognizing the complexities and the scars, and holding them with care. It's a commitment to seeing the other person in their entirety and valuing that wholeness. When respect is woven into the fabric of your relationship, it creates a strong foundation where shadows can be confronted and integrated, rather than left to fester in the dark.

When Abe and I got married and moved in together, I had just rediscovered how important journaling was for me. Due to my mounting depression, it had become hard to communicate with other people, especially him. I didn't know if it was safe to share all the darkness I was feeling, so I wrote it down. I had been holding back so much of myself from him, and from everyone, I felt like a ghost. But as I unpacked the memories associated with the emotions I was moved to write about, it started making sense to me. I began to see it wasn't all hopeless.

I'd go into a little closet we used as an office to write in my journal. It felt like a safe container to sit there and listen to all the voices inside. The more I got it all out, the more solid I felt. I also knew there was another person who deserved to be let into what was going on inside me. It was still too hard for me to talk to him in real time about everything that was burdening me. I'd just choke up and cry, and he'd be left totally confused. So, one day I asked him if he'd let me read him some of my journal.

We sat down together in that tiny office, and I finally showed him all the different shades of misery I was feeling. He saw that I felt small and scared, but now he understood that it wasn't because of him. That first reveal created more space for him to visit me in other dark moments. He didn't have to bring light into my darkness, but just me realizing that I wasn't alone in it was enough. He talked to me like I learned to talk to myself: affirmingly, with love and compassion and understanding. He didn't try to mansplain me out of my gloom, but he reminded me that I was more than what I had been drowning in.

Pride can block relationships with great potential. When searching for and cultivating love, let go of self-righteousness. Ask why. Make an effort to understand. Apologize. Everyone wants love, but few are willing to sacrifice.

Pride can block relationships with great potential. When searching for and cultivating love, let go of self-righteousness. Ask why. Make an effort to understand. Apologize. Everyone wants love, but few are willing to sacrifice.

Zweig married her partner twenty-eight years ago. "We got married in four different spiritual traditions, as well as a ceremony where we vowed to honor and respect each other's shadow parts," she says. "And we knew what they were because we were five years in already. It was not an easy vow to make, but we've healed each other in the most profound ways because we brought that shadow awareness into the marriage." What that looks like on the day to day for them is, "If he says, 'You did this' instead of 'I feel this,' I can say, 'You're blaming, look at yourself.' If I withdraw without communicating, then he can say, 'I'm feeling abandoned by your behavior.' And I can say, 'You know what? I *am* abandoning you. I'm responsible because I couldn't communicate how I felt.' You make it about personal accountability rather than blame."

Benjamin Bernstein and his partner, Spiritsong, have cultivated a similar dynamic. "First, it helps that we are both counselors," he says. "We are both practitioners of our own shadow work. And we're very open and clear with each other. When one of us is triggering, we'll very quickly begin discussing what's happening, the parameters around it, and do the best we can to get clear about what it is that one of us is perceiving about the other. We never feel like we can make a definitive statement about anything. I'll say, okay, I believe that, or I feel that, but neither of us is going to pronounce God's absolute truth to the other person. We both understand we're subjective beings. And if one of us needs to do some more shadow work, we can hold space for the other to do it, or even facilitate it for the other if it feels appropriate."

For experienced shadow workers, this is exemplary. For mere mortals, Zweig suggests, "Give each other time. A lot of people can't do this when they're highly reactive. If there's a big shadow charge in the moment, and you can't necessarily do shadow work on it right there, you need to rely on yourself to calm down and self-reflect."

In *Monsters in Love*, Menakem designed what he calls "the five anchors"—activities to help stay conscious in a moment of relational distress that happen to be excellent shadow work tools:

"Soothe and resource yourself first to quiet your mind, calm your heart and settle your body," he writes. "Pause, then notice and discern the sensations, vibrations and emotions in your body instead of reacting to them. Accept and tolerate the discomfort instead of trying to flee from it. Stay present and in your body as you move through the unfolding experience, with all its ambiguity and uncertainty, and respond from the best parts of yourself. Metabolize any energy that remains."[6]

"Where love reigns, there is no will to power; and where the will to power is paramount, love is lacking," Jung wrote. "The one is the shadow of the other."[7]

If we are lucky enough to find a significant other, sharing our lives calls us to be vulnerable and forgiving.

If we are lucky enough to find a significant other, sharing our lives calls us to be vulnerable and forgiving. Holding another person's heart in your hands without breaking it is a blessed responsibility, and it is done more fluidly and naturally when you have already learned to hold your own with grace. Love, in its purest form, is an act of surrender, not dominance. In many forms, love is sacrifice. It requires the courage to let go of control, to let the heart lead where the mind cannot. As you learn to embrace your own shadows, you open the door to a love that is free from fear, a love that allows both you and your partner to grow in the light of true understanding. This is the kind of love that doesn't just hold, but uplifts.

SIX

THE SOCIAL SHADOW

If my mom is born, as a Black woman, into a society that predicates her body as deviant, the amount of cortisol that is in her nervous system when I'm being born is teaching my nervous system something. Trauma decontextualized in a person looks like personality. Trauma decontextualized in a family looks like family traits. Trauma in a people looks like culture.

—RESMAA MENAKEM, IN AN INTERVIEW WITH KRISTA TIPPETT, *ON BEING* PODCAST[I]

Up to now, we've mostly looked at how the shadow works in personal, intimate, and family settings—how when we find a way to meet our shadow with love and acceptance, we create space for authentic healing, intimacy, inner strength, growth, and joy.

Our larger society has a shadow function too, one that is bigger than any individual. It's impossible to avoid. Greed and brutality run the show far too often in our big world, making it easy for us to simply assume that might makes right. We are bombarded by violence in the news, and then we go seek out more in TV and movies and games. Nobody would want to live in the conditions we broadcast to ourselves as entertainment, all day, every day. Sex without love is everywhere, flattened out like some kind of prize. We worship antiheroes and fuckups and criminals in fiction—and then we shun them in real life.

The collective shadow is mostly beyond our control to radically alter in our lifetimes, so the payoff of working with it is harder to grasp in the present. But what we do today absolutely affects how the social shadow expresses itself for generations to come. Understanding that social transformation usually takes longer than a typical human lifetime, shadow work is still a valuable tool for helping redirect the human stream, one person at a time. It also helps us find clarity in how we withstand the world's influences and handle its challenges.

Charting the intersections of the world's shadow and our own can help each one of us find a more natural place in the firmament and approach global problems with more love and compassion. This makes us stronger, more resilient, and better equipped to positively affect our communities.

Shadow work has a huge role to play in detoxifying what kind of social beings we are. You read in the previous chapter about how being more conscious of your shadow material helps you stop projecting in intimate relationships. The same is true outside the home. "Projections change the world into a replica of one's unknown face," Jung wrote.[2] Grappling with your shadow will change how you see the world and how you show up in it too.

Shadow work has a huge role to play in detoxifying what kind of social beings we are.

We have much incentive to hide from ourselves and others on the social stage. In trying to be nice, good, just, politically correct, and in line with our community, whatever its values and priorities, we sweep a lot under the rug. Jung was not cute or naive about the depths of the shadow. Inside everyone is the capacity to become a tyrant, a narcissist, a brute, a demagogue. Inside everyone's shadow lives prejudice and intolerance too.

Some people even feed into it, bringing it out of the dark and reveling in their hate. In doing shadow work, we talk a lot about acceptance and nonjudgment, but the ultimate point isn't to simply give vent to our most monstrous selves. We love them as unhealed parts of us and recognize that they have something valuable to teach us. In learning from them, not ignoring them or wishing them away, we defuse their worst potentials. We don't wallow in them.

I can promise you that what comes up for me in dreams and active imagination is not always peace and love. I have been birds and been wrapped in the wings of angels, and I have become an outcast and transformed into a dragon and burned down whole villages. The unconscious is wild, and I continue to thank myself for creating a larger and more open space to peer into mine, while trusting myself to act in my daily life from a wiser and more constructive place.

This chapter will cover three poles of society and the shadow. The first will show how keeping your own shadow garden well-tended can keep you from falling into social shadow traps of fear and resentment. It can help decrease any knee-jerk tendency to overidentify with a particular tribe, or scapegoat out-groups. It can help create breathing space from our current political polarization, which so easily makes enemies out of fellow humans. It can help us become more sensitive to our seeming inability to mitigate mass suffering. That one is an especially big heartbreaker—but as we have explored in previous chapters, heartbreak is always also an opportunity.

Shadow work can help puncture any false sense of superiority that comes from the racism, sexism, sizeism, ableism, and all the other -isms that haunt our institutions, which deny common humanity to everyone else. It can help you become more compassionate toward those who fall through the world's cracks: refugees, addicts, the homeless and mentally ill, whom so many larger structures like to render invisible, out of sight in denial. And if "fallen through the cracks" describes where you are in your life right now, know that shadow work can help you find the authentic strength and self-love to rise up.

We'll also discuss the impact of shadow work for future generations, to transform the traumatic inheritance of our human history and help leave the world a better place than how we found it. The radical forgiveness of shadow work is contagious. It's a crucial step to being able to see others from the same nuanced and loving perspective through which you learn to see yourself. I believe that even if you do only this, and nothing else, the result can move mountains. But there is more to consider.

The third part of this chapter will offer some examples of engaging productively with the social shadow to confront problems on a larger scale—examples that depart from ideology-first dogmatism, out-of-balance heroism, and ego-first savior complexes, while leaving space for imperfection and the fullness of humanity. These examples are not the same as individual shadow work, but they share an orientation of radical honesty, fluidity, acceptance, and compassion. They prioritize collaboration across our obvious differences. They are here to inspire you and to show that when we're aligned with who we really are and extend our hearts to others, each of us has unexpected power.

No matter where you stand on the spectrum of political belief, how you work with others makes a difference. We are more effective in the world, more in sync with our communities, and more available to inspire and help others without burning out when we tend to our shadows. If political activism is where your passions take you, we'll also touch on what to stay conscious of in your shadow (and your group's shadow) as you get involved. Shadow work helps you embrace passions and positions in a cleaner and wiser way, whatever those positions may be.

Remember that to heal something, it must be fully known and understood. Even as we need to construct boundaries around our informational intake, something we'll look at in the next chapter, we cannot look away from suffering and expect it to get better on its own. Also remember that there is always hope. It lies in you and me and all of us stepping into the greatness of who we can be—something that can happen to the fullest only when we embrace and work with our shadows. Doing my own shadow work eradicated apathy in me and vastly increased my capacity to have faith in the goodness of others. That's the most crucial ingredient of all if we want to make the world a more loving place.

Fear of malice blocks faith in goodness. Where our fear tells us "what if . . . ," our faith responds with "even if . . ."

Fear of malice blocks faith in goodness. Where our fear tells us "what if . . . ," our faith responds with "even if . . ."

Society, like our families, contributes enormously to the reservoir of shadow material in all of us. It starts to affect us the minute we're born—some might even say before. Even if we didn't understand larger world structures as babies, we sensed their strictures in the stress of our parents as they struggled with institutions and other people. We picked up from our earliest moments in life that no matter who we are, in the eyes of the bigger world out there, our color, our gender identity, our family's accent, and whom we love aren't neutral. We started to see where we stood in the larger order of things and adjusted our consciousness accordingly. This is true for those of us whom society considers exemplary and fortunate, and everyone else too.

We also started to see, while we were still young, the hypocrisies and inconsistencies of what people say versus what they do, in public opposed to in private. We absorbed the gains and losses of leaning into ego and persona to solidify a place in the world and the disappointment of double standards. We saw that the world was extremely complicated and could be a minefield, intersecting our most intimate relationships. We weren't entirely wrong, though we didn't have the whole picture.

The world shadow enmeshes itself into our human form through no desire or will of our own. I remember one afternoon when I was twelve years old. It was a hot August day. Middle school was just starting back up, and I wanted to walk there alone. It might have been the first time I was allowed to do so unaccompanied, and I was excited to feel my own independence. I wore denim Bermuda shorts and my favorite Limited Too T-shirt. "Girls Rule," it proclaimed. Nice idea, not so much the reality.

I felt the sun on my skin as I skipped along, enjoying my brand-new freedom and the freshly planted rosebushes growing on the sidewalks. Back-to-school signs were everywhere; neat, fresh notebooks were still on sale at the drugstore, perfumed by the faint scent of eraser rubber; brand-new backpacks hung in windows. By the time I got to school and sat on the floor, crisscross applesauce like the teachers had told us to, an older boy whistled at me lasciviously. Then he came up to me, sat down next to me, glued his left hip to my right one, and pressed himself against my small body. He was twice my size.

"You're so pretty . . . your legs feel so nice . . . you look so sexy . . . ," he said to me, as if from another hormonal planet. I jumped in my skin and felt exposed, scared, and ashamed. Why was he making that aggressive, sexy come-on at *me*? I wasn't trying to be sexy. I was twelve. That was for big kids like him, or adults, really. That shouldn't have concerned me. I was frozen in shock and felt sick to my stomach.

When he got up and walked away, my prayers felt like they had been answered. But I still wished I could go back to those rosebushes and jump into them to hide, even as I went about my day at school, trembling, with my little head held high, pretending to be brave, feeling like a lamb in a den of wolves. I didn't want to walk home alone when the day ended. My newfound sense of freedom and safety was stripped away from me that morning.

I told my mom what happened when I got home, and she told me that the best thing to do in the face of bigger boys like that was to laugh at them. That might have been perfectly fine advice woman to woman, even if what underlies it is sad as hell. But I was twelve, and there was no way I was going to pull that off.

I didn't know how to ask for it, but more than words, I needed her to hold and contain and comfort me as I felt my understanding of the world turn on its axis in the space of five minutes. Neither of us could change how the world preyed on girls in that instant, but we could have managed the intrusion of that savagery a little better.

After that day, anytime I felt like a boy was approaching or hitting on me, I would shut it down as if automatically and put on my best bitch face. Sometimes I would go further, pulling a grim mean expression, to repel them before they got too close, so they wouldn't come nearer. I was like a cat, hissing at any glance of approach or interest. Looking back on it now, it was a little extreme, but it did work.

That was just one introduction I got to living female in America. Kids are always trying to make sense out of things, and so, worried that I had somehow attracted this out-of-bounds behavior—because my brand-new evidence taught me that being joyful and free in the big world meant becoming a target of sexual aggression and assault—I put a piece of my confidence and capacity for joy into my shadow that day.

My Innocent took a huge hit before she was ready, like so many other children have experienced in the world. (Maybe all of them, in their own ways.) I started to develop defenses that hardened into a bitter-tinged shell, sedimented over, layer by layer, from many other instances of unwanted male harassment throughout my life—always when I was just minding my own business, enjoying myself. I know many other women who have versions of this tale.

Every boy and girl who grows up Black or another ethnic minority in America has stories of how they have been harshly treated by the bigger world simply because of their looks or culture. Or misunderstood, not trusted, or given the benefit of the doubt. Every kid who grows up gender nonconforming, or in a differently abled or "oversize" body, knows what I'm talking about too. Many of their stories will be more violent than the one I just told. All of them are complex and formative.

There is kindness all around us, and we have a soul instinct to find it and grab onto it. If we are vulnerable to the social shadow as humans, especially when we're young, we also have an incredible capacity for resilience and growth, which we'll dig into more fully in Chapter Eight. Healing from the punches and kicks and abuse that come from living is possible, and indeed part of thriving in the world. Even if we all need to form boundaries and learn self-protection as we mature, it always comes with a cost.

Shadow work can help you recover some of the softness you had to sacrifice. And in honoring yourself and your emotions, you create a more empowered space from which to operate.

For me, shadow work was crucial to reuniting with my twelve-year-old self, to letting her fear and disappointment and panic resurface without recrimination or laughter or explaining it away. I needed to revisit and feel what I was encouraged to bury then and mourn that loss of freedom once more in my body and in my heart, not just my head. It was still down there even if I tried to ignore it, and even still when I simply intellectually understood it. It was time I dug in deeper.

Journaling, active remembering, and meditation were how I got there. I remember how much I cried when I put myself back into my young skin at school that day. At one point, I beat my chest like a gorilla and roared to express the anger I had at that kid, and all the countless others after. (I still do that every now and again when I am alone and feel any kind of anger or tension well up—it feels great to let it rip.) I needed to get all that heavy energy out of my body as much as my soul.

And then, exhausted, I comforted myself like I wished I had been comforted long ago. Repeatedly, I would close my eyes and breathe deeply, visualizing taking that twelve-year-old girl into my arms, telling her that her fear was natural and normal. (Repeatedly is key here—one of the interesting findings of Internal Family Systems therapy is that our inner wounded parts need proof of our love, care, and nonjudgment to trust us and unwind. We can't just say it to them, we have to show them over and over.) I would tell her that now, today, I am a big grown-up who knows much better how to protect herself. But that whenever she is afraid—because she still lives and breathes inside me—she is safe to pour her fear out to me. I pledged to her that I would never diminish it or laugh it off, and that I would always take her seriously and have her back.

The close attention entailed by shadow work helped me inhabit that memory from all sides. As I entered a space of deep compassion for myself, I was able to naturally extend that to my mother's reaction. She had her own stories of assault when she was young. It was in journaling, responding to a prompt about vulnerability, that I connected the dots to things she had told me through the years. A time when she was followed to her car and a note with a compliment was already attached to her window. Another time, when she was quite young, a neighbor tried to lure her into his home with candy. The way she wouldn't allow me to sleep over at anyone's house—not even my closest friends'. "You'll understand when you're older," she would tell me, except I never really did. I could see that her urging me to toughen up and laugh was her wanting me to survive what she had survived without falling apart, and that her influence on little me to dissociate came from her own still-wounded place. She was doing the best she could.

That exercise made it easier for me to identify other wounded places in my mother that at other times in my youth made it hard for her to be there for me in the ways I needed her to. (Even the best parent is imperfect, as we all are.) All this movement in my life rippled out from going back to the site of the original wound, over moments of intense reflection; letting my memories, my unconscious, my once-buried emotions, and my body all speak; developing a loving relationship with that terrified twelve-year-old girl and holding us both with care.

It is a blessing if we can do this together with our families. "I had a great talk with my father about twenty years ago, before he passed, and he said the most amazing thing that just shook me," recalls Jock, sixty-one, an African American man teaching drama in Barstow, California. "He was a military man, not one to apologize. But there he was, apologizing for not creating a better path, not taking chances, not doing things in life that would make our generation a little smoother. And I thought, man, I've got to change. The main thing I want to do is break those cycles that plagued my family for years. Our religious background, society, school, even my parents made me feel extremely guilty about having dreams or desires. We've got to believe that we're just as worthy, just as deserving, and just as capable of manifesting greatness as the next person."

Jock started journaling, fill-in-the-blank exercises, and doing mirror work by himself. Now he and his daughter have created a dialogue around shadow work together, sharing exercises with each other, and strengthening their family bond actively. This not only helps reverse painful family traditions, it also forges healthy new ones. It can feel scary at first—I know that when I first shared my journal with my husband, I practically held my breath—but like compassion, courage is contagious too.

Jock's and mine are just two examples of how larger society, combined with social wounds in one person, can create a fertile climate for them in their kin. And how attention, care, and a willingness to explore those wounds while keeping the faith made new flowers bloom where the ground might have stayed barren. It speaks to shadow transmission, and healing, through one generation, from my mother to me, or two, from Jock's father, through him, to his daughter. Now imagine millennia of that, layers and layers of pain and residual trauma, just waiting to be unearthed and properly beheld.

Human history is one of tribes and tribalism. While the support of the tribe allowed people to take on more complex tasks and evolve, the obvious downside is in how we too often dealt with other tribes. We've been fighting, raping, pillaging, kidnapping, invading, enslaving, and killing each other practically since human society has existed, transmitting the soul scars down through the ages. Even though our tools have gotten fancier and average standards of living have risen, comparatively, our collective present has some major evolving to do.

Even if we don't have a conscious memory of what befell our ancestors, we carry their experiences in our bodies and in our unconscious minds. We are the repositories of what they lived, not just in our collective unconscious, not just in our conscious cultural stories, but in our cells and DNA too.

Even if we don't have a conscious memory of what befell our ancestors, we carry their experiences in our bodies and in our unconscious minds.

In Chapter Three, we looked at how trauma lives in the shadow and in the body. Our bodies are storehouses of how society has played with us, our families, our communities, and our species across time—meaning, all the racial trauma, sexual violence, terror, bullying, and humiliation experienced by our ancestors carry down to us too.

The emerging science of epigenetics quantifies it. Epigenetics studies how the environment can also alter our genetic expression via a cluster of chemical markers, especially when we're young. These chemical markers can control which kinds of stress hormones get released when we're triggered. They affect our temperament, and they're as inheritable as DNA itself.[3] The implication is that unhealed trauma is hereditary too. It echoes in all of us.

It's overwhelming when you think about it, knowing that we also carry traces of our ancestors' mindsets and fears and hard lessons. Our families have passed down prejudices, and suffered from them too, through generations. Prejudice is a soul wound for the person expressing it as much as it is for the object of it. Shadow work is a courageous way to own up to and surmount that without self-hate or writing yourself and your people off for being imperfect. Of course you're imperfect. We all are. There is power in grasping how deep the sting of ancestral suffering goes. There are effective tools to help heal this and the -isms that live in all our shadows. There are concrete things we can do to stop the cycle, create more space and freedom, and show others how to achieve that for themselves too.

For Resmaa Menakem, whose insights on relationships informed Chapter Five, prejudice is centered in the amygdala, what he refers to as the lizard brain in his book *My Grandmother's Hands: Racialized Trauma and the Pathway to Mending Our Hearts and Bodies.* "Our lizard brain only understands survival and protection," he writes.[4] "All our sensory input has to pass through the reptilian part of our brain before it even reaches the cortex, where we think and reason. Our lizard brain scans all of this input and responds, in a fraction of a second, by either letting something into the cortex or rejecting it, and inciting a fight, flee or freeze response."[5]

Menakem's book compiles research on generational and racial trauma and offers techniques for healing it that I would define as shadow work, going beyond well-meaning (and still-important) cognitive exercises to focus on somatic exploration, memory, and active imagination. Menakem reminds readers that no matter their lineage, they have inherited brutality. The charge that we all still carry from that, even if it happened millennia ago, informs how we live in a diverse world today.

Menakem's book offers an impressive array of mindfulness exercises. Each one is different, but each centers the body's responses to racialized stressors and comforts, and each asks the reader to discover what they need to do to ground and return to steadiness. In one, readers are encouraged to lay down a circle of safety around them physically, using a string or a cord, and then visualize different kinds of people with different kinds of body language crossing into it, and track what responses that brings up in their bodies and what their bodies want to do next.

The only way to find the oasis of peace is in passing through the desert. Alda Sainfort, MD, OMD, MDiv, is a family lineage healing practitioner based in Miami, Florida, who works with clients to access generational blockages. Diagnosis starts by feeling her client's pulse, a technique she learned studying Chinese medicine and Ayurveda. "In the Eastern system, when we're feeling the pulse, we are feeling the internal organs, the emotions, everything related to the person," she explains. Sainfort is also, like many intuitives, able to sense her clients' emotional pains and blockages in her own body, so she uses how she feels physically in a session to help guide them.

As she works to isolate issues, Sainfort will ask clients about their family histories: "Is there anyone in your family you notice with that same emotion? Do you know if your grandparents suffered the same?" She encourages clients to inquire with their relatives, but she can work even without concrete, conscious information by asking them to access their unconscious mind and generational memory through visualization.

"I was doing a healing for a young lady whose ancestors were from the Czech Republic," she recalls. "And I clearly saw this man. I asked her if she did too, and she did. 'I have no idea who that person is,' she told me. I told her to ask him his name. She got it, and then she investigated her genealogy. I think he was seven or eight generations back. Now we wanted to connect with him, to ask him what happened." Using guided active imagination, "he told us, 'I had to kill a lot of people to survive,' and some of the methods were very unpleasant. We were able to work with that."

The next step is clearing the generational emotional chains, which is a hybrid process that depends on the patient. Sainfort works as a medium and guide during the process, having designed a protocol using sacred Sufi mantras, visualization, and directing patients to sing or scream, growl, or cry for release.

People can work on their own to access their ancestors, too. Many religious traditions have carved out a conscious space to remember their forebears in daily life. Even if you don't come from one of those, know that even your subtlest inheritance—familial, emotional, or communication patterns; phobias or assumptions—is real and there for you to access and heal. Sainfort has offered the following exercise for guidance. Embellish, add, tweak, and adjust according to where your spirit or intuition may take you:

1) Identify which side of your family you want to work with: paternal or maternal. Take one side at a time. Hold what you know about these ancestors lightly in your head and strongly in your heart. "Think of a characteristic thread, something you've noticed is repeated on that side of your lineage," Sainfort says. "It could be trauma, depression, or difficult circumstances."

2) Start deep belly breathing, five to six counts per in and out breath. Do this for a few minutes until you feel yourself fully inhabiting your body. Like with mindfulness meditation, if your mind wanders, let the thoughts glide by; don't attach yourself to them.

3) Create an imaginary circle in your mind. "You can make it as large as you want," Sainfort says. Invite your ancestors to step inside: the parent you wanted to work with, their siblings, their parents and grandparents, going back twelve generations. "Even if you never met them, they will come. They love to be acknowledged and are always ready to come when we call."

4) Picture them arriving and pay attention to how they show up. “Are they feeling happy? Sad? Is anyone limping or in a wheelchair? Feel it in your body too and notice where it’s showing up.”

5) Call on the parent, or the primary relative you need the most healing with. Visualize yourself taking a step forward and facing that person. Notice how your body feels. “Whatever relationship you have with them, now is not the time to judge that,” Sainfort notes. “Let your heart open and connect with them and notice if you feel any resistance. Let it all happen.”

6) Now ask for forgiveness. For Sainfort this isn’t the kind of forgiveness that you seek when someone has done something wrong. It’s simply a presencing of everyone, their shadows and wounds and dramas included, in the light of awareness and love.

7) Next, Sainfort offers an Arabic mantra you can repeat while breathing deeply and holding the whole family circle in your heart: *Astagfirullah al-Azeem.* “It means, ‘I am returning my heart to the almighty through repentance,’” she says. “Feel your heart opening to be a container for your whole family lineage.”

8) If another relative also shows themselves to you clearly during any part of the process, repeat the steps above with them, whether you recognize them visually or not, continuing to pay attention to any sensations in your body. “You can physically open your arms to them if you want,” Sainfort adds, “to help them feel forgiveness too.”

9) Lastly, imagine the whole family group holding hands together in a circle. Feel the love and strength that radiates through your palms from them and to them.

No matter what our family situation, lately we've all had a lot to heal from. The Covid-19 pandemic shut the world down to experience panic and loss in relative isolation, and I don't believe we've adequately come to terms with the damage that did to us collectively. This is a big reason why I became an advocate for shadow work and decided to write this book. We've mostly wanted to turn away from what we experienced together—the mass death, the loss to families, the justifiable dread of the headlines, the intense fear of the unknown—to brush ourselves off and move on.

That is a missed opportunity to ask many important questions. Do we turn away from suffering, especially our awareness of other people's, because in it we sense our own powerlessness? Because it just seems too big? Or too messy? Or contagious? The courage that shadow work engenders can help us understand what is so uncomfortable in us in recognizing our own vulnerability first. Could it be that nothing but a twist of fate or luck separates us from them?

Don't look away.

Don't look away.

One of the most effective ways to encourage recognition and compassion on a mass scale is through inspiration. There is something about music, especially, that raises the vibration. Music is the shorthand of emotion. It can engage the intellect or not, but it always speaks directly to the heart, whether you're a listener or writing and performing music yourself. When we're in a bad way, the heart is what helps the most. Many people have a favorite song that has helped them get through the worst of times.

During pandemic confinement, the country artist Jelly Roll (real name Jason DeFord) became a bard of society's shadow outcasts, particularly the addicted and the incarcerated. The son of an opioid addict who struggled with anxiety and depression, he became an addict himself and started dealing drugs at age thirteen. He loved music and was starting to make a name for himself as a rapper around the Nashville area where he grew up, even if most of the time he was in and out of jail.

It was on a potential twenty-year stretch that he learned he had become a father. Not being present for his child's birth fired up his will and ambition to change the course of his life. That led him to discover his singing voice and the depths of emotion it allowed him to reach in himself. Jelly Roll was shy about singing at first, but soon he began writing intensely personal ballads about addiction and loss, like his mother's and the mother of his daughter's, from the point of view of the fallen, the sinners, the hopeless.

A brief aside: though Jelly Roll clicked into something larger than himself by developing his singing voice despite his fear, his power doesn't come from the particular aesthetic or style of creative expression he uses, but from how fully his heart and soul are engaged to alchemize that shadow material, both his own and the larger world's. If you want some of that to a hip-hop beat, try not to bawl your eyes out listening to Kendrick Lamar's "Mother, I Sober," where Lamar wrestles with the lineage of his mother's sexual trauma, on his transcendent album *Mr. Morale and the Big Steppers*.

Different genres take on specific aspects of the human experience and societal conditions. A lot of hip-hop explores struggle, resilience, resistance, systemic oppression, and social injustice. Country music gives a lot of time to narratives of heartache, loyalty, and the quest for simpler times, reflecting the socioeconomic challenges of rural (mostly) white America. Pop music, with its wide appeal, often glosses over deeper issues, but it can capture the zeitgeist of the moment, echoing the audience's collective joys, fears, and fantasies. "The best music is essentially there to provide you something to face the world with," Bruce Springsteen once said. Another bard of the forgotten, he should know.

During confinement, when so many in dysfunctional homes found no relief, when substance and domestic abuse skyrocketed as the world faced an unknown disease that struck hardest at the most precarious, Jelly Roll recorded "Save Me," a ballad of simple, piercing clarity that captured the feelings of shame and powerlessness of addiction while praying for deliverance. He uploaded it to YouTube in May 2020, and it became a hymn for millions trapped inside the double prison of their homes and their demons. (At the time of this writing, it has had 242 million views.[6]) People saw themselves in Jelly Roll, covered in tattoos, with a totally different physique from the commercial country world's glitzy airbrushed perfection. (In 2015, he weighed five hundred pounds.) Like many an inspired voice, he made people feel less alone in their despair by honoring their weakness and struggle.

"I'm like a scared child when I have to sing," he says in the documentary *Jelly Roll: Save Me*. "Maybe I'm a decent singer because I don't know how to sing. I'm the one dude singing songs for the broken. This community has allowed me to speak on their behalf. On behalf of the depressed, the stressed, the anxious, the addicted. I'm just documenting what I see and what I know. I've been a drug addict. I've been a loser. I've been a stealer."[7]

In that documentary, Jelly Roll goes on a concert tour. At night he performs for audiences with touches of an old-time church revival meeting that echo his Southern Baptist upbringing. During the day, he visits jails, juvenile facilities, and rehab centers. He performs for inmates and patients. He does a lot of compassionate listening, holds space for grief, and urges people not to give up, reminding them that if he can rise above, they can too, if they commit to themselves.

"Music meets us where we are," he said in a 2023 appearance on *The Daily Show*. "Music is therapeutic, it's there to help and heal. It's a constant in a life that doesn't have many constants."[8]

To that end, Jelly Roll helped fund a music center for the inmates of the Davidson County Juvenile Detention Center in Nashville, where he once served time.

Now, from a position of commercial success, having won awards and accolades, Jelly Roll shares his personal insecurities and ongoing struggles with substances and his weight freely with his enormous social media following, fiercely motivated to destigmatize human imperfection by example. In this way, he's a model of how to go into the world in a public way while owning his own shadow and honoring everyone else's.

It is only right to use your influence if you have it. Touching souls through art is one way. Politics is another channel, but it comes with caveats. We may have the noblest thoughts for our fellow men and women, but we must remember that politics—organized action taken to restructure institutions—comes with its own forceful shadow. That shouldn't scare you away from engaging if you feel the call, but it needs to be recognized.

"If we disown our anger, our racism, our impotence, our narcissism, our violence, and then we see it reflected outside of ourselves, it has a lot of charge," says Connie Zweig, whose book with Jeremiah Abrams, *Meeting the Shadow: The Hidden Power of the Dark Side of Human Nature*, includes whole chapters on social groups and enemy making.[9] "Groups are identifying with each other in a fanatical way now," she continues. "The expression is different, and the values are different, depending on the political group in question, but they're identified with their tribes. And when you identify with a group, whether it's a church or a Sangha or a political party, very similar dynamics happen. There's a charismatic leader, there's a desire for rescue, a desire for belonging and to have enemies. Somebody's shadow starts acting out for whatever reason and the group is mesmerized, and it becomes a collective psychosis. We're engaged in shadow projection when we hate certain politicians and give our power away to others."

Shadow Projection Exercise

1) Ask yourself who your political enemies are. Pick the worst example you can find, your most hated elected official or other powerful leader. The one whose face makes your stomach turn and whose voice alone sets your teeth on edge and makes you see red. That person may indeed have made some decisions that are demonstrably awful, but the emotional charge you bring to them is yours and yours alone. Understand that you are projecting.

2) Now go deeper into that material. Make a list of those traits, the ones that upset you the most.

3) Sit with your grievance list, understanding that those traits exist in your shadow too. Referring to Julianna Rees's technique from Chapter Three, using your body and all your senses to bring an emotion to life, do it on this list too. What do the charged qualities you attribute to this person feel like inside you? Where does it feel activated in your body? What does avarice feel like? Hatred? Malice? What color do they have? What texture? What temperature? Investigate.

4) Now take out your journal and explore what you find in writing. Or if you prefer visual engagement, do some active imagination. Focusing on the activation in your body, get quiet, and let free-floating images come. This is your unconscious peeking through to teach you that there is always much, much more to a grudge.

Here's another suggestion, from Rainn Wilson, that recalls the "empty chair" technique from Chapter Four. "You can engage in a dialogue with all these different aspects of yourself," he says. "You can do it in a journal, or just do it. I used to do it with my therapist, like playacting in the room."

Set up an empty chair and sit opposite it.

"Into that chair you put, like, your inner resentful teenager, or your dark addict that wants to fuck everything up," Wilson says. "And then you have a conversation. I would go sit in the chair and be controlling Rainn or narcissistic Rainn or scared nine-year-old Rainn, and I would go back and forth and continue the conversation."

Let them be as unreasonable as possible. "I'd say to myself, 'Fuck you, you're an idiot, so shut up!' Get to that stuff, because then you can go, 'Oh wow, there's a part of me that really hates myself.' It unveils so much about who we are and the forces that drive us."

Jung was pessimistic about politics as a space of fulfillment. For him, one of the biggest pitfalls of the modern world was how it transforms individuals into a mass, like statistics, with no human uniqueness. His writings toward the end of his life were filled with angst about how twentieth-century political systems, both in the West and under powerful communist states, crushed people and reduced them to mere data. "Under the influence of statistical assumptions, not only the psyche but the individual man and indeed, all individual events whatsoever suffer a leveling down and a process of blurring that distorts the picture of reality into conceptual average," he writes in his screed of an essay, "The Plight of the Individual in Modern Society." "We ought not to underestimate the psychological effect of the statistical world-picture: it thrusts aside the individual in favor of anonymous units that pile up into mass formations."[10]

Even when you're in a privileged position in relation to large, institutional power structures—if you are an Ivy-educated white guy, or lucky enough to own property, or are a successful rock star—for Jung, the structures built to organize society restrict people's personal freedom and sovereignty all the same. He believed social healing began with healing individuals, helping them rise above, among other things, modern undifferentiation. We need "inner, transcendent experience which alone can protect [man] from the otherwise inevitable submersion in the mass."[11]

But it's hard to make the case for living with awareness in the world today without wanting to make a change to it somehow—and to be fair, Jung never argued for apathy or inaction either. He believed shadow work was a moral imperative for individuals and for the good of the world. He never said you should stop at your own front door.

When you are strong and solid in yourself, you can be a more effective change-maker. "I go to therapy. I take it very seriously," Jelly Roll said in that *Daily Show* interview about what keeps him on track. "My relationship with God . . . And more than anything my search for purpose. I quit searching to be happy and I started searching to be useful. And that's when everything changed for me. . . . I tore people down for decades and I want to lift people up."

When you are strong and solid in yourself, you can be a more effective change-maker.

Zweig told me about the shadow work she did on a part of herself she calls "the judge": "I was looking at the consequences of me identifying with my judgment and I felt really separate from people. I had this ego need to feel superior, but once I started working with the judge, what happened was, my heart opened. I began to feel much more empathy, more patience with people, more interested in people, not only looking for people who were just like me."

A crucial ingredient to moving through any social problem—from intergroup conflict to war—is forgiveness, which can take root only through collaboration and radical honesty. This is something you see on an international scale through a political process called Truth and Reconciliation.

Truth and Reconciliation Commissions—whether in post-apartheid South Africa, post-genocide Rwanda, post-dictatorship Argentina, or in Australia and Canada, to address the violence toward and abuse of indigenous people—weight restorative over retributive justice. Rather than solely assigning consequences to perpetrators, the focus is on repairing harm and restoring community, including a peaceful return to life for those guilty of crimes. Common to all such commissions is giving the participants in a conflict—both perpetrators and victims—the space to speak openly to each other. Victims confront abusers directly, with the understanding that only by a full reckoning with events can a community live together again without more deadly conflict.

These commissions are not without controversy. They don't satisfy everyone.[12] Forgiveness is a big ask. To institutionalize it requires transparency and ongoing maintenance so that old wounds do not continue to cause social chaos. It never works perfectly, because it requires all parties to change their fundamental perception of themselves. But it is incumbent on them to try, and in trying, already there is improvement.

Pumla Godobo-Madikizela is a South African psychologist who

served on South Africa's Truth and Reconciliation Commission, which was first set up in 1996. She contributed an essay to a *New York Times* series in 2024 seeking answers to the question "What do we fear?" Her answer was that we fear forgiveness. There is a lot at stake: for surviving victims, there is the fear that in giving up vigilance, atrocities might be forgotten. But for Godobo-Madikizela, forgiveness is also the only way to transform the past rather than repeat it.

"Maybe the thing we fear most is that by forgiving, we might be relinquishing our power and giving it to the recipient of our forgiveness. Or do we fear the uncertainty of what might come after forgiving—could forgiving simply condone what happened, throwing the hope of reconciliation into chaos? Is it thus easier to cling to the familiar terrain of violence and dehumanization instead of creating conditions that might foster human bonds with others?

"The psychological and moral flexibility required for a forgiving gesture—even when one's internal compass points in the opposite direction and the offender seems undeserving—is precisely what prepares us to imagine a reality in which we begin to heal. It also helps us consider the journey of the person we're forgiving."[13]

Like anything else in life where the stakes are high, politics is risky business. On the ground level, it can mean stepping into a mess of ego projection and power struggles. With money and prestige at stake, it is easy to fall into corruption too. "Right now, every system in the world is based on competition and profit," says Rainn Wilson. "You name the system: criminal justice, agriculture, education, certainly the political system. If you talk to any expert in those fields, they'll tell you these systems are really broken. They're based on one-upmanship and backstabbing, and every man for himself and corporate profitability and the seeking of power. And this is unsustainable. So how do we create systems based around love? For a lot of people, that's a naive quest. But I believe that we can harness the spiritual being-ness inside all of us to make our interactions and our systems ever better.

"If we live with maximum compassion for other beings, then we can't live with ourselves if there's so much suffering going on. So, we have to harness our talents, our faculties, we have to sacrifice our time, our energy, our comfort, even our social status to help others. That's why it's really important to be doing shadow work. We do our internal work so that we charge our batteries, go out in the world and try to make the world a better place. And as we do that, we charge our batteries more so we can serve more."

Here's another idea of what that might look like one day down the road, courtesy of Thich Nhat Hanh, the late Buddhist monk and peace activist, in a 1993 speech to close out a day of mindfulness. "It is possible the next Buddha will not take the form of an individual," he said. "The next Buddha may take the form of a community, a community practicing understanding and loving kindness, a community practicing mindful living. And the practice can be carried out as a group, as a city, as a nation."[14]

Nhat Hanh's is a beautiful vision to hold on to. It is not just a pipe dream, either. Emily Cutts, a Glasgow-based community activist, recounts leading an urban renewal campaign that turned into a grassroots well-being movement in her memoir, *The Dear Wild Place: Green Spaces, Community and Campaigning.*[15]

From a distance, Cutts's story might look like a standard NIMBY crusade—she was fighting to reclaim a derelict, grown-over vacant lot, the North Kelvin Meadow, between one of the most economically deprived neighborhoods in the city and one of its poshest, from a big residential development. But what Cutts was looking to establish there was not a manicured park or a botanical garden but an honest-to-goodness small wild forest, and the way she went about it made all the difference.

Through existing neglect, trees had already grown back enough to have fostered a small ecosystem in urban Glasgow. But the place had started to feel dangerous to locals, who used it mostly as a place to let their dogs soil without cleaning it up. Cutts had to overcome not just moneyed interests but also the pessimism of residents who either feared or didn't see the importance of untamed nature. And she had to butt up against the culture of "safetyism," which discourages independent outdoor play for kids.

In her book Cutts assembles reams of research on the benefits of spending time in nature: how it reduces stress, depression, and aggression; assuages ADHD; reduces brain activity related to obsessive rumination; and even brings in vitro benefits to fetuses. "Wild space can help people to know themselves," Cutts writes. "It can also bring people out of dark holes and give meaning and purpose in a sometimes scary world."[16]

The nonlinearity of a proper forest, one that grows and changes on its own naturally, uncontrolled by humans, is a prime place to access those nonlinear wild places in ourselves. (Just ask a sylvotherapist. The practice of forest bathing, called *shinrin-yoku*, first came to prominence in Japan in the 1980s as an antidote to burnout.[17]) Cutts adopted nonlinearity in her organizing style too. "The key issue in my mind was that an academic argument based on planning policies would not be enough to stop this multi-million pound juggernaut," she writes. "I was convinced that only an empowered community, in love with the land, could have a real effect. And to do this, citizens from near and far had to get on the land, use it regularly, and begin to develop that deep affection for it."[18] That meant hosting play groups and creative writing sessions in the woods, throwing Halloween parties, and organizing treasure hunts.

After Cutts managed to stop the building, she kept reaching out. She went to the local McDonald's, which had become a hangout for at-risk boys seen by locals as untouchable menaces. Little by little, she won their trust enough to get a few to come around to the woods, eventually tailoring an outdoor program with Venture Scotland to teach them canoeing, climbing, hill walking, and mountain biking, for school credit. Now she has expanded to work with several other local schools. Cutts also established a community garden, with classes, that reaped more than just vegetables. "One woman who comes to our gardening club suffers from depression and appreciates the fact that she can drop in and out depending on how she is feeling and that there is no pressure to come every week. . . . This is the beauty of community activities—they are there for you if you need them."[19]

What makes Cutts's efforts contagious is how horizontal and imperfect they are. In organizing, she notes the importance of distributing leadership to encourage a sense of collective responsibility. "Do things in a makeshift/do-it-yourself kind of way," she writes in a how-to section on community building. "This gets away from business as usual perfection and increases confidence in others. If you can show someone how easy it is to do something, and not have standards that are too high, it might inspire others to do it too."[20]

Love of the land is something we all must cultivate if we want to help save the planet from ecological disaster. If I am neutral on political ideology as it pertains to shadow work, I am not neutral on the importance of developing a greater respect for nature. Splitting ourselves off from it was one of Jung's most fervent worries about modern humanity. Mother Earth is one of the most potent archetypes in the collective unconsciousness. Taking her out of the center of our souls separates us from our own wildness and strength. "One of the biggest problems that eco-psychologists identified from the beginning is that humans don't feel we're part of nature," Dennis Merritt tells me. "James Hillman, one of my favorite analysts, said that pathologies around the environment are going to make us aware that we're part of it because if we screw it up so badly that it starts to affect us, then we must be part of it."

Love motivates the stickiest action, like the evolution of Interface, a globally distributed flooring company. In 1994, founder Ray Anderson had an ecological awakening, pledging not just to drastically trim his company's carbon footprint but to allow nature to inspire its future growth and development. Employees and investors fled, but he doubled down, hiring scientists and thinkers to analyze the movement of natural ecosystems. They rethought carpeting according to how leaves fell on the forest floor, reinvented production techniques, and reset the template for the industry.

There is no such thing as achieving perfection. It's the nature of our being, the nature of our existence to strive for it, but we never attain it. When confronting the shadow in society, it's crucial to remember that our domain is in continuous, incremental changes in how we live, consume, and interact with the world around us. It might also mean fostering a deeper connection with nature, acknowledging your role within it, and striving to protect it.

There is no such thing as achieving perfection.

How you see the planet is revealing. It's like that viral blue-or-gold dress meme that everyone fought over for a week. Some of us are wired to see blue, and some are wired to see yellow. The planet is there to be exploited, or it's there to be healed. What does that say about how you see yourself? Or your parents? Or any source of nurturing and sustenance in your life?

When I was in college, my roommate had this Frisbee sitting

upside down on the counter of our kitchenette. I looked inside its saucer shape and saw she had filled it with glitter. At first I was disgusted: there was hair and fuzz and dust in there. But then I took a step back and realized I was looking into a completely improbable object custom-geared to another dimension of play. How cool is that? I leaned into that spirit and looked at it again, with curiosity and awe. The overhead light made the glitter shimmer and glimmer, with fractals of colors bouncing in all directions. It was a party inside that Frisbee. What disgusted me the first time enlightened me the second time.

So, when you look at the world and consider the state of it, ask yourself what you go to first. It's easy to look at the complexity of the problem and throw up your hands. Do you see it as a monstrous system of oppression with no way out? Do you notice every piece of litter, every leaf curling into brown, everything decomposing? Or can you see the bees dunking their tiny heads into flowers, recycling pollen, spreading life by being life?

Is it one reality? Yes. Is it the other? Yes. Is it everything in between? Absolutely.

In each of us there is a great capacity for love, which means we're halfway there already. Remember that in reaching into your shadow, you are reaching into your own untamed forest. The chaos and the power there still beat to the rhythm of your own heart. Which is the rhythm of the world.

SEVEN

THE TECHNOLOGICAL SHADOW

The Internet suggests immortality—comes just shy of promising it—with its magic. With its readability and persistence of data. With its suggestion of universal connectedness. With its disembodied images and sounds. And then, just as suddenly, it stirs grief: the deep feeling that digitization has cost us something very profound.

—VIRGINIA HEFFERNAN,
MAGIC AND LOSS: THE INTERNET AS ART[1]

Scroll . . . scroll . . . look up . . . scroll . . . Have you ever caught a fleeting moment of awareness between scrolls and wondered how hypnotized you must appear, glued to the endless stream of content on your phone? Looking up and around feels like surfacing for air after being underwater, taking a deep breath of another time and place—a place of physical presence and awareness of your immediate surroundings that was once all we knew.

On my second honeymoon in 2022, my husband and I traveled to Thailand. During a three-hour layover in Singapore, I watched a group of monks bowing their heads. Were they praying together? No, each one was deeply entranced by his phone. I was in awe. It really does get to the best of us.

This moment served as a powerful reminder: even those dedicated to a life of mindfulness and presence can be swept away by the digital tide. I know I still can.

In a world designed to distract, finding moments of genuine connection and presence is a revolutionary act. Embrace those pauses, breathe deeply, and reclaim the richness of the world around you. Remember, true awareness isn't about avoiding technology but about mastering its influence on your consciousness.

In a world designed to distract, finding moments of genuine connection and presence is a revolutionary act. Embrace those pauses, breathe deeply, and reclaim the richness of the world around you.

Technology's rate of development, and our adoption of it, has grown asymptotically, like an ever-intensifying upward curve. Before we have time to get used to a new mode or medium, we move on to something else. Social media is one of the loudest examples of the intersection of technology and daily life, a place where our unacknowledged selves find expression in the digital ether, where our desires for recognition, love, and validation meet the parts of us that feel unworthy—and for the whole world to see. It hasn't even been with us for twenty years.

To take an example of this disruption from just one sphere: Where once we had legacy institutions to dispense information about the changing world, today social media and internet search have displaced traditional news, substituting loud and catchy extroverts, or SEO wizards, for credentialed and fact-checked expertise. Too often, what gets to be considered true is now down not to who knows the most, but who yells the loudest, makes you laugh the hardest, or paid the most for the promotion. In that and many more ways, the digital world is a new playground for a new power differential. Of course, our shadows come along for the ride.

There's lately been a powerful movement toward authenticity. The endless parade of fakery on social media is wearing us thin. Shadow work is like a deep, cleansing breath, stripping away the masks we wear, urging us to embrace our true selves. This raw honesty fosters deeper, more genuine connections with others. It's about showing up as who we really are and finding liberation in that truth.

I think that one reason *The Shadow Work Journal* resonated so much online was that it wasn't about becoming your best self but embracing your worst self. To truly grow, we need to understand our darker sides. The way forward is often backward. It's an internal journey, not an external one. There are no expectations, no judgments—just mindful awareness. It gives you permission to be who you are when no one is looking. Aren't you curious?

As opposed to rosy-eyed utopians or downcast doomers, I believe that wherever we have a human endeavor, which technology is, we have gray areas, mixed results, questionable motivations, and also unlimited potential for evolution and spiritual progress. "When you invent the ship, you also invent the shipwreck," wrote the philosopher Paul Virilio. "When you invent the plane, you also invent the plane crash; and when you invent electricity, you invent electrocution. . . . Every technology carries its own negativity, which is invented at the same time as technical progress."[2]

The rise of new technologies is yet another opportunity to better understand our shadows, and the world's shadow, on a fast-evolving terrain. The crucial difference is that technology externalizes your attention, harvesting it for profit and power. Shadow work internalizes your attention, channeling it into growth and resilience.

In this chapter we'll talk primarily about the shadow online: how it adapts to the digital world and how you can remain aware of yours and others' while trying to stay afloat in the rushing infostream. If there is a lot in the data on how we adapt to digital conditions that feel like crisis, Taoist wisdom proves itself once again: in crisis, there is opportunity. I'll also present a catalog of online-specific archetypes, a sort of digital-world twist on what we looked at in Chapter Four. We'll dive into the mental health risks of social media usage—which we all need to understand, given how much we engage—but we'll also take a good look at its extraordinary potential. Mindfulness is everything when you're living day to day in this Wonderland, so I'm also including several simple exercises to help with that.

It's up to each of us to carve out a space to thrive in the age we live in now. This has always been our lot, since our earliest beginnings as a species confronted, time and again, with our game-changing innovations. And now here we are once more at the dawn of a new age, like we were before with the camera, the printing press, the wheel, and fire. I take this history as proof that we are all more than capable of rising to the occasion.

In his day, Jung sounded an alarm: writing about the atom bomb, he said that technology was outpacing our ability to evolve alongside it. "One must ask oneself whether man is sufficiently equipped with reason to be able to resist the temptation to use [technology] for destructive purposes, or whether his constitution will allow him to be swept into catastrophe."[3]

He worried that technological speed would mean we wouldn't have the time to reflect on the profundity of our dreams, imagination, and ruminations. This potential disconnection from our inner selves would prevent us from being able to truly understand ourselves. It's hard to see how he was wrong about speed and reflection, at least. The pace of modern life is so fast it's like we're on a psychic crash course fueled by distraction and amped-up reactivity. Our brains are wired to chase constant stimulation, and the digitized world is nothing if not a dispenser of dopamine hits from notifications, emails, and closing tasks. They bring the fleeting satisfaction of feeling masterful, even if we resemble lab rats chasing cheese more than the sovereign beings we really are.

We must admit that we have become entirely entangled with our devices. This not only disrupts our sleep, cutting off one of the surest routes to the unconscious, it hinders intimate connection to the people around us. In *Burn Book: A Tech Love Story*, the journalist Kara Swisher recalls, "I had taken to joking at the end when I made speeches: 'I leave you to your own devices. I mean that: your phone is the best relationship you all have now, the first thing you pick up in the morning and the last thing you touch at night.'"[4]

But I don't think Jung foresaw how, like any other human endeavor, interconnected technology shows us to ourselves so blatantly. Therein lies the potential of it, if we approach it with wisdom and compassion.

Since its earliest days, the internet has been a canvas for our hopes, complaints, capacities, fantasies, tastes, and obsessions. "The Internet favors speed, accuracy, wit, prolificacy, and versatility," writes Virginia Heffernan in *Magic and Loss: The Internet as Art.*[5] "But it also favors integrity, mindfulness, and wise action. For however alien in appearance, the Internet is a cultural object visibly on a continuum with all the cultural artifacts that preceded it. . . . It is not outside civilization, it is a new and formidable iteration of that civilization. It's also a brilliant commentary on it." In short, it is us, refracted through a fast-changing prism.

Our days may increasingly drift away from shared physical spaces and real-time exchanges, but wherever we go, even into virtual realms, we carry ourselves along. Our childlike fear of the unknown and our insatiable curiosity are mirrored in how we approach new platforms. We expose our wounded desire to be seen, loved, and approved of when we post selfies. Our unspoken urge to dominate and win fuels battles of ideas on Facebook, TikTok, and Twitter. The vulnerability we mask is evident when we ghost others on dating apps.

We see our shadows in our device addiction, using seemingly more controllable synthetic experiences to distract from real-time interactions with those right there in the room. Every time we pick up our phones, we send a message about who and what we are choosing. Cultivate an awareness of these patterns. Recognize the reflection of your deeper self in your digital habits. Let this insight guide you back to more authentic and meaningful connections.

If one of the most knee-jerk ways we have of handling shadow material is to project it onto others, social media provides an optimal terrain for blasting what we don't own in ourselves out onto everyone else. Shadow work is an excellent tool for treating the digital realm as another mirror in which we can get to know ourselves better. By inviting our shadows to the table more consciously, our use of technology has a better chance of becoming an empowering experience rather than an unconscious compulsion.

New technologies may be destabilizing to old norms, but they also have huge potential to enlighten. We must know ourselves, to be able to put that bedazzlement, and that sometimes desperate yearning for connection, onto healthier and more solid ground.

A mantra to affirm: "I release the need for constant distraction. In this moment, I choose presence, I choose peace."

A mantra to affirm: "I release the need for constant distraction. In this moment, I choose presence, I choose peace."

To enact this, we need to be cognizant of just how much the digital world bends our lived experience. In the infinite scroll of updates, posts, and notifications, time seems to shrink, stretch, and sometimes disappear entirely. Events from years past resurface with the immediacy of recent memories, while the constant influx of new content makes yesterday's news feel ancient. This disembodied landscape, where past, present, and future collide in a continuous stream, challenges the traditional rhythm of how our lives pass. Recall the last day you spent hours scrolling—you were delirious by moonrise, weren't you?

The immediacy and perpetuity of digital interactions foster a sense of urgency and instant gratification that puts us on edge. The desire for instant responses, the expectation of constant availability, and the pressure to keep up with an ever-accelerating newsfeed can make time feel both infinite and scarce, while we dog-paddle in off-kilter discomfort. This unique condition of digital time (not to mention the blue light emitted from our screens) disrupts our internal clocks and, really, our internal selves.[6]

This is a space of instability on many levels—mind, body, and soul. Usually disruption makes us reach out, like the small children we once were, to whatever is closest that feels good. Online addiction is a closed-loop response to this epistemically shaky ground. Like all addictions, it is an outlet for unfulfilled emotional needs, a temporary balm for loneliness, boredom, and feelings of chaos or inadequacy. We are seeking soothing in the very thing that is riling us up. What is that about?

Social media platforms are designed to exploit these vulnerabilities with little accountability.[7] We are learning more about how they tweak algorithms to draw us to bombast, drama, and discord. "Platforms often incentivize conflict actors toward more divisive and potentially violence-inducing speech, while also facilitating mass harassment and manipulation," found a 2023 study by the Knight First Amendment Institute.[8] "Facebook, as well as Twitter and Google's YouTube, have become the digital arms dealers of the modern age," wrote Kara Swisher in a 2018 column for the *New York Times*. "They have mutated human communication, so that connecting people has too often become about pitting them against one another and turbocharged that discord to an unprecedented and damaging volume."[9]

The data is overwhelming that excessive social media usage is linked to decreased psychological well-being. Studies have found causal connections between the time spent on platforms and a rogue's gallery of agonies: disordered eating and poor body image, depression, anxiety, psychological distress, and increased incidence of alcoholism.[10] Social media usage increases the anxiety we feel about our looks and lives, leaving everyone—especially girls and women—more desperate for outside validation.[11]

One possible hope—which would probably make Jung turn in his grave, because of his suspicion of purely political solutions—is in regulation and limitation, because too many of us are unable to separate ourselves from the source of our addictions without the hand of a larger authority. (Remember that Steve Jobs wouldn't let his kids use the gadgets he created.[12]) Jung would have argued that it was in all of us to individually rise to the occasion, but let's be realistic. The mass effects of unhealthy platforms are too consequential to let faith alone take charge.

Today, countries all over the world are starting to consider smartphone bans in schools. There is reason to think it's the right call. One boarding school in Buxton, Massachusetts, swapped smartphones out for "light phones." Light phones are larger devices with only black-and-white screens. Phone calls and slow-paced text messages are the only kind of person-to-person communication possible, with rudimentary map functionality and some capacity to play music.

"Most everyone agrees . . . that the school is better off without these hell devices. (And yes, that includes students.)," wrote Tik Root in the *Guardian.* "There are fewer interruptions during class, more meaningful interactions around campus, and less time spent on screens. 'It's a problem we've found a pretty good way to address,' Scott Hunter, who teaches English and music, said of smartphones. Bea Sas, a senior at Buxton, added: 'I think people are a lot more social.'"[13]

This story gets to the irony of all this connectedness and immediacy: how alone it makes so many of us feel. Even before lockdown, the world was undergoing what several national health organizations have called an epidemic of loneliness, exacerbated by digital conditions. Loneliness is not the same as solitude—it doesn't feel like a choice to recharge, but an abandonment by others, a lack of available connection and support.

A study on loneliness conducted by US Surgeon General Vivek Murthy sent him out on a nationwide listening tour. "Even when they couldn't put their finger on the word 'lonely,'" he noted in the introduction to his findings, released in 2023, "time and time again, people of all ages and socioeconomic backgrounds, from every corner of the country, would tell me, 'I have to shoulder all of life's burdens by myself,' or 'if I disappear tomorrow, no one will even notice.' It was a lightbulb moment for me: social disconnection was far more common than I had realized."

Murtha's grouping of the data was illuminating. Between 2003 and 2020, people's alone time increased by twenty-four hours a month. They decreased time spent with friends by twenty hours a month. For people between the ages of fifteen and twenty-four, the figure is even more pronounced: in-person time with friends decreased by nearly 70 percent.[14]

This shift challenges us to rethink how we connect and what we value in our interactions. Are we losing the essence of community in our pursuit of digital engagement? The solitude we find ourselves in can be a fertile ground for self-discovery, yet it also begs the question:

What are we sacrificing in the process?

There are significant health consequences to loneliness, including a greater risk of cardiovascular disease, dementia, stroke, depression, anxiety, and premature death. "The mortality impact of being socially disconnected is similar to that caused by smoking up to 15 cigarettes a day, and even greater than that associated with obesity and physical inactivity. And the harmful consequences of a society that lacks social connection can be felt in our schools, workplaces, and civic organizations, where performance, productivity, and engagement are diminished."[15]

When we're vulnerable, sensitive, and feeling adrift, we're more easily manipulated. If there were ever a collective moment that defines that state, it was the Covid-19 pandemic and the global lockdowns that brought an unprecedented level of isolation and uncertainty. New communities were formed in cyberspace during that time, new support systems that started to grow roots too. But in the urge to seek solace and find answers online, some of the most psychically vulnerable among us were easy marks for radicalization and conspiracy theories. Extremist activity online rose markedly.[16]

"The internet does not cause radicalization," observed a cross-disciplinary study on the effect of online influence networks, "but it helps spread extremist ideas, enables people interested in these ideas to form communities, and mainstreams conspiracy theories and distrust in institutions."[17]

Conspiracy theories are shadow projections that seek to simplify complex problems by implying that some all-powerful force is in control. As the world continues to tumble into chaos, these rabbit holes bring a feeling of cognitive order by positing that there is one true answer to all the disorder and injustice, out there to be uncovered if only you keep looking. Online wormholes are a place where deep-seated anxieties and fears are redirected onto an unfolding mystery that the theorist community can help try to solve, like heroes in a strange imaginary spy movie.

By acknowledging and exploring your shadow in your online world and how you come into other people's, you can transform engagement from a source of distress or unfulfilled longing into a catalyst for growth.

By acknowledging and exploring your shadow in your online world and how you come into other people's, you can transform engagement from a source of distress or unfulfilled longing into a catalyst for growth.

Start with the basics of your presence on social media: the internet offers a kaleidoscope of opportunities to chisel and hone personas. The temptation is mostly too strong not to. The curated lives of others that we encounter on our feeds, the constant comparisons we make to highlight reels masquerading as everyday life, set unrealistic benchmarks for success, happiness, and beauty, further entrenching our own feelings of inadequacy. They make us feel less than, left out, or longing for a life that seems just out of reach, propelling us deeper into the very shadows we try to escape.

Need validation? Share your accomplishments. Feeling invisible? Post a selfie. Don't feel pretty enough? Add a filter. Feeling insecure? Post a thirst trap. With image technology evolving, our online exchange has become a giant fun house mirror, with an emphasis on code-switching and two-dimensional avatars. And so, we sign up to flatten ourselves too and then color in the lines according to what we want to be true, over and over.

Filters, photoshopping, and other tune-ups turn pictures into paintings, not photo reality, allowing not only for stunning creativity, but also new levels of fakery and trickery that set people up to be defensive in exchanges with new people.

We become sleuths of the strangest signifiers—a few key words in a profile, a kind of hat or jeans or the message on a T-shirt—as if those abstracted codes could really speak to a whole human. Forms of exchange are abbreviated, leaving an enormous amount of blank space on which to project fantasies or nightmares onto another. We often leap to fit digital strangers into a preconceived position. We suspiciously search for holes, or we too innocently wish that a relative stranger with only the fuzziest outlines will become the new answer to our prayers.

Remember that if all personas are constructed to appeal, they also conceal shadows of equal or greater power. I'm pluralizing it on purpose, because many of us craft a new one for each platform. Many people have alternate accounts, some for their upstanding public faces, like their LinkedIn self, if you will. And then they have an anonymous account, or several, on a chat board or gaming server, where they channel their darkest selves, their inner shitposter or killer or nihilist or troll.

We may once have done this in concrete spheres of existence—separating who we show up as depending on the arena. But now we can multiply that effect, leading to far more complex fragmentation, and express each facet without leaving our desks. There is an unhinged anarchy in this, a spirit that can embody the literal meaning of carefree: without care. This new split introduces a fresh sense of what's permitted and what isn't. It requires careful attention to how you navigate it. In this digital age, we all become creators and influencers, regardless of our roles in society. The way we inhabit this space shapes how we self-identify in profound ways, for better or worse.

The ultimate creative act is the art of crafting your own self.

The ultimate creative act is the art of crafting your own self. We all participate in this charade to some degree or another, and it doesn't make the ground feel solid beneath our feet. What an opportunity to examine those alter egos! To mindfully track what you feel free to say and post, where, what part of you is doing it, and to what end. This is valuable information about how you sort through and inhabit your online world—which is becoming the place where most of us spend the majority of our time. Think of it as your inner algorithm.

As to the outer algorithms, the ones we encounter on social media and in search, they understand us more than we might understand ourselves. Whether in the hands of a platform looking to manipulate your behavior or not, an algorithm tracks your digital footprint, compiling a comprehensive profile of your online behavior, connecting the dots to follow your internal direction, creating a never-ending run of information that tweaks your internal chemistry. It is an unbiased observer, devoid of emotion or preference other than to get you to engage, operating solely on the data you feed them through clicks, likes, shares, and the time you spend lingering over a post. This feedback loop continually refines its understanding, becoming more precise with every click.

This dynamic between user behavior and algorithmic response is a lot like the Law of Attraction, which posits that what we focus our energy on grows. This is similar to the reinforcement theory as well, which holds that our behavior is shaped by its outcomes. Positive experiences encourage us to repeat actions, while negative ones push us away. As our thoughts and feelings bring corresponding experiences to us, algorithms operate on the principle that content we engage with dictates what we're shown next. If we gravitate to what's positive and uplifting, the algorithm will present more of the same. Conversely, if we're drawn to negative or polarizing content, our feeds will reflect those choices.

We know that littering is a visible blemish on our environment, something that detracts from the collective experience of beauty and peace. Yet when it comes to our presence online, we often forget that our actions can leave similar marks—less visible, perhaps, but no less impactful.

Technology and online spaces are like the shared parks of our society's consciousness. Each time we engage, we leave something behind—our thoughts, our words, our energy. And just as with littering, what we leave behind can either contribute to the cleanliness and clarity of these shared spaces or clutter them with negativity and projected shadows.

Avoiding this digital litter requires mindfulness. It's about showing up without dragging our unresolved baggage into the space. It means being aware of our shadows—those parts of ourselves we haven't fully dealt with—and resisting the urge to push them onto others. It's easy to unload our frustrations, fears, and insecurities in a place where we can remain anonymous, but doing so is like tossing garbage out the window as we drive by. It might feel good in the moment, but it leaves a mess for someone else to deal with.

Just as we carry a responsibility to the physical world, we also carry a responsibility to the digital one. When we encounter someone else's shadow online—whether it's in a comment, a post, or an interaction—there's an opportunity to respond with compassion rather than react from our own shadows. This doesn't mean condoning harmful behavior, but it does mean recognizing that the person on the other side is wrestling with something, just as we all are. By responding with empathy, we help clear away the clutter rather than adding to it.

The goal isn't to be perfect, it is to be conscious. We can choose to be part of the solution, not by suppressing our shadows but by acknowledging them, understanding them, and not letting them dictate our actions. Consider this and the following questions to avoid contributing to society's technological landfill of shadows:

What shadowy aspects of yourself are currently being projected onto your feed? How can you take more conscious control over the digital environments you inhabit?

What shadowy aspects of yourself are currently being projected onto your feed? How can you take more conscious control over the digital environments you inhabit?

Ask yourself what thoughts and emotions you're repeatedly feeding. If a friend's vacation photos trigger envy, reflect on why that is. Is it your own longing for adventure? Are you feeling left out? Inadequate? Alone? Note that, don't bury it.

Shadow work is self-excavation. You're the archeologist of your inner world. Introduce digital mindfulness into your shadow work journey as an exercise in intrapersonal intelligence.

When you have conversations with yourself, you hold up a mirror to your mind and get a never-before-seen point of view. You'll see what's really going on there, backstage. When something you see in cyberspace seems to shimmer especially brightly, there's your projection, and there is your task. Is this shiny object catching your eye from its authenticity? Keep it close to remind you of how it's reflecting your own essence back to you. Or is it something that's engaging your shadow? Look at what part of you and why and decide if you're ready to let it go. You'll start to get the hang of this process the more you get used to conscientiously conversing with yourself.

As you navigate your own feed and others', you should also pay special attention to one of the most important focal points in any digital self-presentation: the profile picture. If the eyes are windows to the soul, then profile pictures are the irises of our online personas. The choice of one goes beyond mere aesthetics; it's a declaration of identity, a silent communicator of aspirations and inhibitions.

Psychologists and online body language experts (who are in some ways like modern-day fortune tellers) delve into the nuances of profile pictures, uncovering layers of personality, hidden desires, and unspoken fears. Like reading tea leaves for the digital era, this can make for a fascinating blend of self-expression and psychological revelation, where the chosen image—whether a candid snapshot, a carefully curated portrait, or an abstract avatar—serves as a window into the complexities of the individual behind the screen.

The colors, composition, and recurring themes in our digital representations carry symbolic weight. These visual cues can point to the shadow aspects we haven't fully acknowledged in ourselves. In this light, the seemingly simple act of selecting a profile picture becomes an exercise in self-awareness and introspection.

Digital Mindfulness Exercise

1) Look at your own profile pictures with fresh eyes. Take a good few minutes with each one and reflect on what you're communicating in each. Are you adopting the confident pose of the Ruler or the thoughtful gaze of the Sage? A penchant for nature shots could represent an Explorer's craving for freedom and discovery. If you remember from Chapter Four, anytime we shift into an archetypal expression, we have an opportunity to see if we are embodying its shadow form or its higher-vibrational one. Whenever something is being brought forward, something else is being masked. What are your pictures hiding that you need to bring to light and embrace? What about the undersides of your confident or joyful poses?

2) This is a perfect subject for a journaling prompt. Take each one of your social media accounts—anonymous and named—and dig into what each one is there for. Where do you emphasize your good boy or girl, and how? What do you hide behind another face and why? Are you embarrassed to worship a pop star if your day job is a position of institutional authority? Why? Are you unwilling to own the depth or fire of your political positions while your uncle is watching, so you create an anon crusader with a cartoon face to slay your enemies? Might there be somewhere else in your life you need to stand up for yourself more? What other kinds of inner saints or villains could you be giving vent to? What other ways might you be investing in your fragments rather than adopting a more integrated self-expression?

3) Know what these aspects of you are. Don't disdain your alters and their masks as merely convenient dumping grounds

of your least palatable urges. Like in the empty chair practice, name these parts of yourself and be curious about the depth and subtleties of who they are. Describe them to yourself as if they were a cast of characters in a play. What are their motivations? Remember, they are your motivations too.

In the age of AI, this shifting borderland between people and machines becomes an even more crucial question. We are at the dawn of an age when computers are deciding more and more for us. While generative AI has been a boon to fields like medical research and diagnosis,[18] for human cultural expression, it's rightfully controversial. AI models come from human-generated data sets. Evidence is starting to mount that they are reproducing human biases too, as in a major feature on AI companies and their inadequate ethical guardrails in the *Washington Post*: "In recently released documents, OpenAI said its latest image generator, DALL-E 3, displays 'a tendency toward a Western point-of-view' with images that 'disproportionately represent individuals who appear White, female, and youthful.'

"Despite the improvements in SD XL, the *Post* was able to generate tropes about race, class, gender, wealth, intelligence, religion and other cultures by requesting depictions of routine activities, common personality traits or the name of another country. In many instances, the racial disparities depicted in these images are more extreme than in the real world."[19]

There are few more direct waking routes to the unconscious than in the act of creativity. The idea that anyone would outsource that to machines is not just risky but heartbreaking. I come from one of the first generations to grow up in an almost entirely digital world, and I accept that we must live in the times and conditions of our age. But giving artistic creation to AI robs us of the most unique pleasure and utility of our species: to question ourselves and, in doing so, to better know our shadows.

If we accept that the internet is a repository of all the light and darkness in humanity, then by definition there are infinite opportunities for connection and healing there. The digital world can knock us for a loop, but in a good way too. Each platform, according to its own rules, fosters communities of support, bringing people together to share advice, encouragement, and resources. These spaces serve as powerful tools for raising awareness, mobilizing social change, and giving a voice to those who might otherwise go unheard. When used mindfully, social media offers access to a wealth of information and perspectives that can broaden our understanding of the world. New kinds of entrepreneurship and community have led to legitimate empowerment and progress.

The synchronicity effect is high in the digital world, too, a rich road into the unconscious. A random Google or YouTube search can change your life. Social media is how I first saw the term "the shadow," in a meme. It was a picture of Darth Vader drinking tea in a field of flowers emblazoned with boxy text that read: "When You Finally Integrate the Shadow."

Memes are a classic example of collective creativity fostered by digital technology across shared platforms. They are the hieroglyphics of our age, a distillation of common experiences and perspectives into compact, usually humorous packages. That shadow meme caught my eye first by making me laugh. And it turned out to be a signpost that profoundly shifted my destiny.

Social media is also primarily how *The Shadow Work Journal* first took off, which helped unlock pathways to healing for—no exaggeration—millions of people. Facebook, TikTok, Instagram, Zoom—it's tempting to look at all these as roads to perdition, but many people have come together in healing communities because of these platforms. Kohn and Amila, whom we both first met in Chapter Three, expanded their spiritual callings through social media and different technological platforms, rippling out to touch exponentially more lives than would have been possible in analog times.

Kohn uses TikTok and Zoom to include virtual group shadow work sessions, creating a vessel for people anywhere with a high-speed connection to show up and support each other spiritually, emerging stronger and more self-aware. Amila, the daughter of Bosnian refugees, first found her spiritual tribe on Facebook because her home life didn't support the awakening she experienced. "Anything spiritual like psychic stuff was forbidden," she recalls. "So, I would join these groups incognito. I just wanted to read what other people were sharing, and it felt really nice to know people were having the same experiences as me." Eventually, the connections she made there were how she started spiritually coaching people, for free. Today she's developed her work into a proper business, dispensing teaching tools and workbooks and giving virtual classes using Google Teach.

By participating in online spaces constructed around mutual growth and positivity, we can collaborate on projects, exchange ideas, and foster a sense of solidarity around anything that moves us. Intentional use of social media allows for mindful engagement and authentic content creation that can hive off like a rhizome, each empowered branch packed with its own potential.

As a social media content creator, producing from my soul instead of from my ego is a profound distinction that resonates deeply within me. There are times when I go weeks without posting because it doesn't feel authentic. Then, there are days when I create ten videos because inspiration overflows, and I feel called to share. My goal with creating Zenfulnote's online platform has always been to create a digital space where you can come as you are, with your mask on or off, and find a place to release and let go of any burdens in your life. Digital sanctuaries foster genuine interactions, even when we're not physically together, and

Zenfulnote's community has been a testament to that. None of us are seeking to annihilate our inner Darth Vaders, but rather to love them for what they reveal about the depths of who we are.

A twist on Jung's archetypes can create another road to clarity online. Social media platforms serve not only as reflections of our individual desires but also as stages for ancient collective symbols. The digital age has simply become the newest setting for their narratives to unfold. Just as each archetype and online persona has its own style of showing up and expressing itself, each also has a unique way of functioning, reflecting your motivations, values, and influences. Here are some examples:

THE INFLUENCER

The Influencer persona, thriving on image-driven platforms, channels the essence of Jung's Ruler archetype. With every post and story, Influencers feed the demand for new trends, commanding attention and inspiring their dedicated followers. Leadership here is measured in likes and shares. In terms of money and power, these are the new online royalty.

THE ACTIVIST

The Activist online embodies the Warrior's spirit, fighting valiantly for justice and change using platforms as swords to cut through apathy, champion causes, and protect the vulnerable. Sometimes, the Activist can succumb to "slacktivism," where the ease of online support—such as signing petitions or sharing content—does not translate into tangible, real-world change.

THE CREATOR

The Creator persona online resembles the analog Creator, except it uses social media as a canvas to express beauty and innovation through their own body. These digital artists transform virtual spaces into galleries of their imagination, sharing their art, ideas, and visions with a global audience. The shadow side emerges when the quest for originality leads to isolation, or when the pursuit of online validation overshadows the intrinsic value of the work, leading to self-censorship or flat commercialism merely chasing digital applause. In this shadow, the digital Creator may find themselves chasing trends exhaustively or altering their authentic voice to suit fleeting tastes, losing a piece of their authentic soul in the process.

THE CURATOR

Like the Sage, the Curator's role is to spotlight meaningful ideas like a digital librarian, enlightening, educating, and inspiring their followers. Through a discerning selection of articles, images, videos, and conversation, they offer digestible knowledge in a sea of informational overload. The shadow appears when what is shared becomes more about personal ego than enriching collective consciousness. Here, the Curator may prioritize content that bolsters their status rather than genuinely seeking to uplift and inform.

THE EDUCATOR

Another iteration of the Sage, the Educator offers straightforward guidance, knowledge, and wisdom to nurture the intellectual and spiritual development of others. The Educator's shadow emerges when they become dogmatic or biased, presenting personal opinions as universal truths. This can limit the viewer's perspective, discouraging critical thinking and exploration beyond the Educator's viewpoint.

THE REACTOR

The Reactor, most prevalent on YouTube, channels the Jester archetype, entertaining audiences with satire and irony to break down and critique current events and trends. The Reactor's ability to extract humor from drab convention reminds us not to take life too seriously. The shadow side of the Reactor emerges when humor crosses the line into harmful mockery or spreads misinformation under the guise of jokes.

THE CONNECTOR

The Connector is an online version of the Lover, thriving on creating and nurturing communities, sparking meaningful conversations, and fostering connections of value. The Connector's emphasis on bonding, uplifting conversation, and unity echoes the Lover's pursuit of harmony and affection. An overreliance on digital interactions at the expense of real-world relationships is one example of the shadow, leading to superficial exchange that lacks depth and genuine intimacy.

THE SATIRIST

Another guise of the archetypal Fool, the Satirist uses social media to challenge the status quo and provoke thought through clever and often controversially humorous commentary. Masters of memes, they excel at exposing truths, disrupting conventional wisdom, and changing minds by making people laugh. The dark side of the Satirist emerges when critique devolves into cynicism, fostering divisiveness and misunderstanding.

THE LURKER

The Lurker is like a cyberspace Innocent, taking a more passive and observant role in the landscape. Absorbing content without actively engaging or contributing, their silent stance allows them to learn and contemplate, possibly reflecting a desire for simplicity, optimism, and belief in the goodness of the world. On the other side of the coin, passivity can lead to disengagement from real issues, detachment, and apathy.

One of the most effective ways to use social media for shadow work is simply by reflecting on your reaction to what you encounter while you're scrolling online. In the space of a few inches in a comment, people share moments of glory and shattered pain. Which ones make you stop in your tracks? What is your inner world grasping for right now? What is it hungry for? Which narratives are you feeding into? Before letting these automatic thoughts take over, pause and resist the urge to react. This small little break in the cycle allows you to choose a different response,

1) *Set your intention*

Before you begin, think of a unique intention and write it on a piece of paper. Fold the paper into an origami shape—a triangle, a star, or anything you like. Keep this piece near you as a reminder of your purpose during the exercise.

2) *You're an alien; now scroll*

Imagine you just touched down on Earth in a starship. Now open one of your preferred platforms and start scrolling. Look at the posts with curiosity and wonder, as if you are trying to understand human behavior and emotions as if for the first time.

3) *Write down what you find*

Grab a piece of paper, your journal, or open up your notes app. As you scroll, note each time you feel an emotional reaction.

4) *Perform a random act of kindness*

Pause your consumption of online content and get active by engaging in a random act of kindness online. This could be sending a supportive message to a friend out of the blue, donating to a cause, or sharing an uplifting post. Notice how these acts make you feel and how they shift your engagement.

5) *Take a few minutes to assess how it went*

How did time shift when you were scrolling versus when you were acting? What did you glean from what garnered your attention? What do you want to change about it? What do you wish you did more of?

one that aligns more with your true self and your desired state of being. By consistently practicing this mindful engagement, you start to rewire your inner algorithm.

Follow these creative prompts to guide your introspective journey and use the QR code at the end to enhance the experience with visuals.

SCAN HERE

The internet is a giant, multiheaded hydra, but its content is now largely generated by people like you and me. We take so much of online life for granted, as a thing that merely exists, but in fact we are its creators. Which means we need to ask ourselves how we can make our shared space better.

How can we encourage healthier engagement and reduce addictive behaviors? In what ways can we support online creators to ensure they can sustain their work without sacrificing their mental health and authenticity? What steps can we take to foster greater digital literacy, helping people navigate the online world more consciously and responsibly? How can we create online communities that prioritize genuine connection and emotional well-being over superficial validation? What role can educational institutions and policymakers play in promoting a balanced and mindful interaction with digital technologies?

Come up with your own answers here. The path to a more balanced and conscious interaction with the digital world starts with all of us.

EIGHT

INTEGRATING THE SHADOW

The time will come
When, with bliss, you welcome
White light
Such as an open mouth
Invites the first drop of rain
In the dry, ghosted weather
You will have outsoared the shadows
The anger, envy, hate and pain
You will have awakened in them, a new life
Inverting loud disdain
Into quiet compassion
And as the droplets
Descending down
Follow
A child of yourself emerges
With blooming eyes
You will forage a laughter
And hug tightly each other

And every other version of you
"Oh, tender child, why did you hide so soon in the night?
Defenseless and restless you froze in some odd form, of time."
You will blow the dust off the shelf
Of forgotten treasures and troves
And make space
To place yet another mirror down
And watch, with admiration,
The reflection of you,
The unfolding story of your life.

"Integration" is a word that gets thrown around often in the realms of personal development and well-being. I've used it countless times in this book alone. But what does integration really mean? What does it look like, and how does it feel in practice? In this chapter, we'll explore this essential aspect of shadow work from multiple angles. We'll delve into techniques for experiencing integration holistically, turning it into a conscious habit, a second nature, and discuss how it shapes the path of your life ahead.

In the widest sense, integration is the process of evolution. It happens when a snake sheds its skin to reveal a new layer of itself, or when a river carves a path through the landscape, continuously reshaping and refining its course. Integration is at play in the archetype of the phoenix rising from its ashes, a glorious act of rebirth. It's in the annual renewal of how a tree loses its leaves, only to sprout fresh new ones in the spring. Or when you turn a corner to embrace a brand-new life phase of no return, like when a caterpillar morphs into a butterfly, taking on an exhilarating new form.

Nature is the best teacher here. It shows us how to let up on the grip and release and understand that life is cyclical, an ongoing learning process that is truly finished only when your heart has stopped beating. And perhaps it even goes on from there—though that is for each one of us to decide.

We've already seen plenty of examples of integration in the stories and anecdotes in the previous chapters. It's when someone realizes they have up-leveled in some unexpected way. When they click into a new sense of ease and connection. When they act out healthier new patterns without forethought. When they get a flash of inspiration to pursue a new project that never would have felt possible before starting shadow work. When they feel a new desire, unleash a new inner fire, and discover they have more confidence and greater access to the wisdom of their whole self to try achieving it. Its results can't be dictated, but the surprise is often part of the fun. The magic. The alchemy.

The definition of integration that I offer here is different from Jung's. He most often used "integration" to refer to the basic process of bringing urges, feelings, and patterns that live in the unconscious mind into conscious awareness. This is a frequent occurrence when you do shadow work, even from the very beginning, and it is already a big deal. "Becoming conscious of an unconscious content amounts to its integration in the conscious psyche and is therefore a *coniunctio Solis et Lunae* (a union of sun and moon)," he wrote in 1951 in the essay "Alchemy and Psychology."[1] "This process of integration is one of the most important, helpful factors in modern psychotherapy, which is pre-eminently concerned with the psychology of the unconscious, for both the nature of consciousness and that of the unconscious are altered by it."

As if it were alchemy, a great inspiration of Jung's, a new cognitive comprehension of what lives in your unconscious mind means both your ego and your unconscious evolve in relationship to each other. This brings you into greater wholeness already.

But for Jung, the meeting of those two psychic spheres was only the first step. He had observed that individual people could wear their newfound understanding in more and less productive ways. In a 1948 memorandum to UNESCO called "Techniques of Attitude Change Conducive to World Peace," Jung wrote: "[W]e must emphasize that we understand by this the change brought about through the integration of formerly unconscious contents into consciousness. . . . The change is never neutral. It is essentially an increase of consciousness and it depends entirely upon the individual's character what form it will ultimately take."[2]

After a confrontation with their shadow, Jung noted that people could become grandiose and start to believe that they had all the answers. Or they could become depressed and overwhelmed. They could decide they knew enough now and go back to the old routine of projecting their shadow material outside themselves rather than continuing to own it and keeping up with shadow work as their lives move forward. Because it bears repeating: no matter how much shadow work you do, your shadow never goes away. Shadow work helps its grip soften and gives you a chance to turn it into an ally. But your shadow never disappears.

What I'm calling integration picks up where that first flash of knowledge leaves off. It's everything you do going forward: how you wear and inhabit your evolving self; how you make room for your shadow now that you understand it better; what new practices and habits and self-affirming new routines you build in to support your continuing growth. This gives the sparks of insight and emotional release you experience in shadow work the most fertile ground to grow in ways you may never have predicted.

More specifically, as I've come across the term, I've found integration generally refers to two different phenomena.

The first type is consciously pursued and intentionally structured, often following a peak experience with your shadow. This might happen after an intense guided therapy session where you've confronted deep-seated trauma or distressing memories.

The therapist's goal is to help you rebuild your self-esteem and restore a sense of harmony before you step back into the world. Take Brainspotting, for example—the technique I mentioned that uses somatic experiencing and the field of vision to stimulate healing. Therapists who practice it know that certain points where your eyes land can unearth trauma, while others offer relief and comfort. It's like a thoughtful excavation—digging deep to uncover what's hidden—and then carefully filling the hole back up with nurturing soil and water, and directing light onto it so something new can grow.

This kind of structured integration also often happens on retreats or intensives, like the type that Alda Sainfort leads on shadow work and the inner child. Toward the end of the weekend, it's time to "reflect on the healing itself," Sainfort says. She has an array of techniques, but a favorite is letter-writing. "You could write a letter to a specific family member, not necessarily to be sent. Or to yourself, with the intention to let go of a pattern. Often, I have participants release that paper into a body of water, if we're near one, or bury it underground, or burn it, or tear it into tiny fragments to scatter on the wind. We return it to the elements whether we use fire, water, earth, or air, because we are created by the elements ourselves. Nothing is lost, it is simply transformed."

Hans van Wechem and Jeanine Souren have participants, after a high-dose psilocybin trip, draw pictures of resonant images and engage in journaling, but "we also pay a lot of attention to the physical side," says Souren. That means post-trip group sessions of connected breathing—a kind of self-induced hyperventilation—and bonding psychotherapy, which is done all together, with participants pairing off. Partners get as physically close as feels comfortable and rest there together, taking turns allowing whatever deep emotions are triggered by that simple proximity to be expressed and witnessed without the other turning away.

"You see your partner and allow them to see you, and when there is real attention paid, you can see someone's pain, even their background," Souren says. "Some people end up wanting to embrace and get really close to know that whatever comes up is all right and your partner won't abandon you. It's an emotional, corrective experience." Participants are already in a state of heightened openness, and so to cement that with an experience of complete acceptance from another "is also, they tell us, transformative."

These kinds of immersive group experiences can be intensely vulnerable. They might not be right for everyone, especially those who are tender and new to this kind of work, or who have a hard time processing a large emotional release in the company of relative strangers, even those who might become friends. Keep in mind the caveats for choosing shadow work practitioners that we discussed in Chapter One for your group leader too: they need to be doing their own shadow work and have their ego in check. I have heard awful stories: of a shaman who suddenly suggested everyone get naked on an ayahuasca retreat, a "healer" who threw a sexual left turn into the middle of a session with no prior discussion, pressuring the client to act out in the moment. I've heard of retreats where drugs suddenly pop up one night, when everyone is in a heightened state of openness and feeling the magic and not using their best, most pragmatic judgment. Whatever experience you might be considering, whether an experiential seminar over an afternoon or a longer retreat, should honor the principle of gentleness and consent, with intention setting and time for you to get answers to any questions you might have before the work itself gets started. You're there for healing, not to add more trauma.

Go slowly and gradually, but do keep going. "Aftercare is a big part of my practice," says Nicole DeMartine. "You kind of have to close your own loop and take in the frequency you just experienced." She leans heavily on the intense breathwork of Kundalini yoga for processing big realizations, hoping to cement them into big shifts by embodying the change.

DeMartine suggests one exercise known as the "Radiance Charger" that she learned at Yoga Farm Ithaca, a trauma-informed yoga nonprofit in upstate New York. Anyone can do it "to bring both hemispheres of the brain into a state of awareness" after a major internal shift, allowing for a more thorough and balanced integration.

Radiance Charger Exercise

1) "Sit cross-legged," she instructs. "Raise your arms up above your head in a V-shaped formation. Curl your fingertips to the base of your palms and point your thumbs high towards the sky." Imagine it like both your arms are raised in victory, giving a thumbs-up in the direction of the higher self.

2) "Close your eyes, put your attention onto the space just above your head, and do the Breath of Fire for up to three minutes," DeMartine continues. Breath of Fire is rapid in-and-out belly breathing where the emphasis is on pushing out a rapid exhalation, letting the inhalation follow naturally. It oxygenates the blood as it revs you up.

3) "Once you're done, bend your arms at the elbow so your thumbs come down toward your head. Let your thumbs touch right above your crown with your fingers extended to the sky. Take a deep breath, then exhale gently as you let your arms fall back down." Think of it as eating a big meal with a lot of roughage that you're helping go down gracefully.

There is also gradual and ongoing integration that people who have some experience doing shadow work start to notice routinely, almost as if by osmosis.

As it gets more natural the more you do it, integrating shadow material has a dynamic of momentum. "You will notice less judgment of yourself," says Lee Oren. "You will notice that the level of your self-acceptance grows tremendously and sets a tone for your ongoing stability. You may still have triggers, negative experiences, and overwhelm, but you'll be less inclined to personalize them. The need to overthink, correct, and analyze yourself becomes fleeting rather than who you are. It will take time to reframe your negative past experiences in shadow work; they may not feel positive or effective, but the aftermath is."

Natural doesn't mean passive. For Connie Zweig, this kind of integration requires an ongoing exchange and negotiation with the shadow—one that may ebb and flow over time but that is never really finished. "I see it as, when we learn how to center ourselves and observe or witness, or romance, the shadow character, trace its origins in our history, understand how and why it formed and what its needs are, and then begin to actually meet its needs directly, it naturally recedes and has less control over you." In other words, shadow work becomes a practice that you get more fluid and skilled at as you get to know your shadow better and better.

In Chapter Two, we spent some time understanding post-traumatic stress disorder and the shadow. Now let's turn to the related phenomenon of post-traumatic-growth (PTG), a form of shadow integration. Richard Tedeschi, PhD, one of the first psychologists to coin the term, says of experiencing trauma: "We are forced to rethink who we are, what kind of people surround us, what world we live in, and what future we will have. It can be extremely painful. But as research shows, it can also usher in change that will be of value."[3]

The trauma therapist Stephen Joseph, PhD, author of *What Doesn't Kill Us: The New Psychology of Post-Traumatic Growth*,[4] found that 30–70 percent of trauma survivors said they experienced positive changes after a traumatic event, including that their relationships were enhanced. "People describe that they come to value their friends and family more, feel an increased sense of compassion for others and a longing for more intimate relationships," he writes in the British Psychological Society's journal, *The Psychologist*. They also change their views of themselves, "developing in wisdom, personal strength and gratitude, perhaps coupled with a greater acceptance of their vulnerabilities and limitations." And their views of the world can change profoundly too, "re-evaluating their understanding of what really matters in life, becoming less materialistic and more able to live in the present."[5]

For Tedeschi, PTG is usually most efficiently ushered in with therapy, but it can happen in a self-guided way or spontaneously too. He isolates five keys to achieving it effectively: education, or awareness of what you experienced and how it's affected you; emotional regulation, through techniques like mindfulness and physical exercise; disclosure, or talking about it, either with a therapist, a trusted loved one, or in your journal; narrative development, or rewriting your story, which we'll explore further on in this chapter; and service.

Service in the context of PTG means sending healing outward to the collective from the source of the wound—an embodiment of Jung's conviction that we do shadow work for the world as much as we do it for ourselves, and what I will define as light work later on in this chapter. When Fred Guttenberg's daughter Jamie was killed in the 2018 mass shooting at Marjory Stoneman Douglas High School in Parkland, Florida, part of processing his grief meant becoming a fervent advocate for gun control.[6] The day after he got the news, his mission in life changed. Since then, he has authored books, testified before congressional committees, and raises awareness daily on social media—turning the despair he once felt over the ultimate loss into an engine for meaningful change. If only his were a rare story—Guttenberg followed in the footsteps of Congresswoman Lucy McBath, who now represents Georgia's seventh district. After her son Jordan was fatally shot in 2012, she founded Mothers of the Movement, a support and advocacy group for gun control, and eventually ran for office to increase the scope of her mission.

The process of going from traumatic loss to towering strength—a result of integrating shadow work—can be painful and awkward at times. It takes patience with yourself. "The first step is to allow ourselves to struggle," says Michaela Haas, PhD, author of *Bouncing Forward: Transforming Bad Breaks into Breakthroughs*.[7] "Unfortunately we can't allow ourselves to skip that first step. We can't drug the pain away. . . . It doesn't mean we have to struggle all the time, but make space for it."

The process of going from traumatic loss to towering strength—a result of integrating shadow work—can be painful and awkward at times. It takes patience with yourself.

Often as I've gone deeper into my own shadow work, I can be emotionally touchy and reactive for a little while. I cry more easily and often, or I get more tired than I normally would. This is when I take a step back and deploy self-care techniques, like spending some extra time in contemplation soaking up the sun, or dancing, or meditating, allowing myself to just be, without expecting achievement. The honesty, clarity, compassion, and wonderment bundled into this process fill those tears with sweetness. They don't scare me anymore, even if they might require a bit of extra emotional energy.

You know you're experiencing integration when you make a clear and definitive life choice you might not have made before, like leaving an abusive situation. The self-love that shadow work helps facilitate also makes it harder to stay in situations of dysfunction. Upending your life can cause chaos, but even that is its own part of the process: shaking things up, allowing things to fall into a new order and form.

Integration like this sees your humanity as a complex puzzle. The picture you put back together won't be the same as the original one that represented you. It will be a more intricate and harmonious composition than who you are now.

Remember, you are both the artist and the canvas of your life.

Remember, you are both the artist and the canvas of your life.

What does it feel like to find new purpose and inspiration? It feels like flying. As I've gotten to know more people in the *Shadow Work Journal* community, one thing comes back over and over, with every conversation I have about someone's experience doing shadow work: they discover, or rediscover, some kind of creative calling or creative practice. You don't have to be a professional or experienced artist to draw, sing, paint, write, or create. You just have to open the channel of your heart and see if some form of expression emerges. It's a fascinating muscle to develop too. When you seek inspiration, sometimes it's elusive. It plays hide-and-seek, and you begin to look around the room for it, in a color, object, or symbol that draws you into a deeper part of yourself. That search can be its own form of therapy.

Johnny from Texas, whom we met in Chapter One, had been doing shadow work for some months when he spontaneously started welding creatively. He had left a good-paying job in a faraway place to come back home to work on his marriage. That didn't work out, and he found himself living separately from his kids, without a job and with time on his hands. "I have no artistic ability at all," he says. "I have no musical talent. I can tell you some good jokes and I can make you laugh, and that's about it. But I was in my workshop just to stay busy, and I had all these spare engine parts, like bolts and pieces of gears and chains. I figured out I had a welding skill and was able to create some artwork out of it. I put them together in configurations, like hearts and crosses. Symbols. And then my sister saw them and wanted one, and then she and her friends wanted more. I was able to accept compliments on it. It made me feel good about myself. I wasn't expecting any of that."

Johnny dips into creativity because he likes how it makes him feel, not because he's trying to win awards—although there's nothing wrong with ambition. "It's like being in a space where I'm not rushed, and there is a sense of peace in it," he says. "I'm in my element and my environment, and I don't feel like I'm walking on eggshells. I have the freedom to put things where I want them and make them look how I want them to look. And then my son picked up on it and said he wanted to make something for his mother for her birthday, and I was like, 'Okay, come on!' I think that's super-healthy for my kid, too, to reach out and say, 'Hey, can you help me do this?' and I'm like, 'Absolutely, buddy, we'll figure it out.' My confidence level is coming back. I'm okay with who I am and how things are coming together."

As he has made space for himself to create, letting his

unconscious emerge through his eyes and hands, Johnny has also found his emotional temper quieting, his tolerance and patience growing. "I've gone through all these different struggles, from combat to alcoholism, to bad relationships, to being in trouble with the law because I made bad decisions," he says. "I'm falling back in love with life. Now that I can do the work, I am more aware of other people's emotions. In conversations with a sibling or a friend, I'm not as concerned with myself, I listen more, not to respond, but because I genuinely care and can read more between the lines."

The same is true for Destiny, thirty-four, a store manager from Dallas. "As I've done more shadow work, I've seen the walls coming down inside me," she says. "I've learned to be present. Colors are brighter, the sun hits my skin more softly." She never felt inclined to create before, but she has started making digital art and music. "I dress in black, but my art is very colorful. It's kind of like the parts of me I didn't show to the world, but when you see my art now, you see them."

Another unexpected result of Destiny's shadow work was reclaiming her sensitivity and developing extrasensory perception. "My grandmother was a spiritual doctor in Puerto Rico; people used to go to her for healing," she recalls. "I have a cousin who is a medium who used to tell me, 'I don't want to tell you about the gifts that you have because I don't want to influence you. One day when you realize them, you'll come to me.'" In opening herself up to her spiritual birthright, Destiny had to face the ways her mother had contributed to her putting herself into a box. But in treating herself with love, she has been able to extend that love to her mother as well. Doing shadow work "has changed my relationship with my mom," she says.

For Lawrence from New York, whose shadow work path has made him want to become a therapist, the shifting sands of the present moment feel like a blessing. "I had a moment yesterday when I was sitting in the park journaling and thinking," he recalls. "And I wrote down, 'I can literally feel myself changing in the moment.' And it's just a crazy feeling when you can feel your energy shift."

I mentioned before that as I did more shadow work, I took up the flute again. Music has since become one of the most profound ways that my soul takes shape and form. It puts meaning to my feelings in ways I never knew possible. No words, just sounds. No explanations, just intentional noise. No logic, just my loving awareness played out in tonal contrasts. I use music as an outlet for life, allowing me to plummet into the depths of my emotions, to feel the grief, sadness, and joy and to release them. Every song I listen to, every tune I create, is a step toward integrating all parts of myself. It's a bridge to my truth, a reflection of my inner world. Through music, I've learned another, even truer way to embrace my shadow, to dance with my fears, and to celebrate my growth.

Writing this book has inspired me to explore the language of music as a way to give shape and form to my shadow (and my light) through sound. I've created an album that invites you to journey from the depths of darkness to the heights of light. Think of it as a journal of sorts, documenting my personal experiences and reflections on what shadow work has meant to me. You can scan the QR code to listen to this album and immerse yourself in it. I hope it resonates with you and offers another layer of understanding and connection as you navigate your own path.

SCAN HERE TO LISTEN

If shadow work is about confronting the darkness, we do it to transform. One of the most powerful ways to do that is rewriting your story. "Ample evidence shows that shifting how you think about adversity and obstacles positively affects your coping with their impacts," writes Soraya Chemaly in *The Resilience Myth*, a book that asks us to reimagine healing outside the individualistic, heroic, bootstrap mentality so often pushed on us today. "Focusing on redemptive aspects of what you've experienced can reduce despair. When we keep diaries, we engage in similar processing. By writing and rewriting, we project ourselves into alternative outcomes with more deliberation."[8]

Changing your narrative can take many forms, but one of my favorites is through affirmations. These are simple, powerful phrases that we say to ourselves and that eventually we incorporate into our thinking and maybe even share with the world.

Words are vibrations. Vibrations are energy. When we speak, our vocal cords produce sound waves that travel through the air. These are then received by ears and interpreted by brains, first and foremost your own. The energy that your words carry influences your emotions and thoughts. Your body is always listening and looking to match the frequency it is exposed to. Through self-affirmation, you can feed and nourish yourself and bring yourself into greater overall harmony.

Not any old affirmation will do. For it to take hold, it needs to resonate deeply. I've found that the most powerful ones come from shadow work. It's in doing shadow work that you feel your vulnerability and show yourself your wounds. These are the places where you can help build yourself back up.

Wounds are real, and they are the kernels of potential, but they are not the whole truth of us. Rather than identify with the wounding as a forever state, like Tedeschi's call to service, look to your wounds as the source of your transformation.

Wounds are real, and they are the kernels of potential, but they are not the whole truth of us.

One excellent way to compose affirmations is by looking back through your journal for source material. It's there where you share without reservation, where you reveal your deepest suffering. Go back through your entries with an intention to integrate what you find. Maybe the best way to explain what I mean is by showing you one of my own, from 2021, and how I mined it. . . .

> I find myself in different dumps.
> I find myself lost and confused.
> I don't know which path to choose.
> My solution is to take them all.
> Divide myself into 5 and take one step, then fall.
> I fall before I could even taste the glory of doing.
> I fall before I could even find which path is best.
> Will I ever know?
> I have fallen in this hole and got back up never the same again.
>
> I feel like the rest of my life I will live on the lookout. In survival mode. Looking out for holes not to fall in. I'll forget to look at the flowers. I'll forget to look at the sky. I'll forget the way the world was, before that big black hole of a lie.

Reading this back to myself, what stood out were the lost, sad, and disconnected parts of me. I felt broken, even as I saw that I had ambition and desire. With the perspective and distance I gained through time, I recognized that the dumps and slumps I wrote about were connected to each other. My despair was one long thread. Or better said, it was an arrow pointing me closer to the needs that I could later recognize as unfulfilled.

I circled the words that felt, in reading back my writing, the loudest and neediest to me:

"Lost," "confused," "step," and "path" (twice), and "fall" (four times).

In addition to the emotional catharsis the writing provided, the common theme was clear: I needed clarity and direction in my struggle to choose the right path, without being terrified of falling or failing. In my isolation, I was also desperate for connection and support.

So, I composed some rehabilitating phrases that I began to repeat to myself regularly. Because they were tailored to the places in me that needed bolstering, they took hold:

1. I release the fear of falling and failing and embrace the journey with an open heart.

2. I allow myself to feel and express my emotions freely, releasing what no longer serves me.

3. I share my experiences with others, knowing that vulnerability is a strength that builds deeper connections.

The next step was to write a new journal entry transforming this past pain into a story of growth and resilience. Here is what I wrote:

> There was a time when I felt lost and overwhelmed by the weight of my decisions. Every path seemed daunting, and I was paralyzed by the fear of making the wrong choice. I was grieving the path uncharted before even deciding what it would be. It was a period of deep confusion and frustration, where every step forward felt like stumbling into another setback.

> But looking back, I realize that this difficult time was a crucible that forged my inner strength and thickened my skin. It taught me the invaluable lesson of trusting myself and the process of life. Despite the uncertainty, I learned to embrace the journey with all its twists and turns. I discovered the importance of clarity and direction. I discovered the importance of setting a concrete intention. I discovered that decisions are merely there to boost you forward, but the landing can never be planned, and there is a lot to embrace in the unknown.

Affirmations are incredibly simple and, when done right, incredibly effective. I find they are especially so when repeated during mirror work, but there are many ways to practice them, starting with simple, mindful speech and advancing through to chanting and therapeutic meditation. Try what you gravitate to and experiment with the rest if you're curious to branch out.

1) MENTAL AFFIRMATIONS

Mental affirmations are powerful even as they're silent, and they have the added benefit of being accessible anywhere, at any time, useful in situations when speaking out loud isn't possible. Simply repeat your statements in your mind. This is a discreet and effective way to support yourself internally, especially during stressful or challenging times when you feel like it's you against the world. Thoughts like "I am resilient" or "I trust myself" cultivate a continuous flow of positive energy and reinforce a mindset of self-belief and resilience.

2) WHISPERED AFFIRMATIONS

Whispering can be a gentle and intimate way to reinforce positive thoughts, especially in moments when you need a quiet reminder of your strength and worth. Whispering evokes a sense of secrecy and personal connection, and this makes the affirmation feel like a sacred promise to yourself. It works especially well with gentle sentiments like "I am loved" or "I am enough," in those quiet, reflective moments to nurture your inner voice and raise your inner flame.

3) SPOKEN AFFIRMATIONS

One of the most direct and powerful ways to affirm is speaking your affirmations out loud. It engages your sense of hearing and adds an extra layer of reality to your intentions. When you vocalize positive statements about yourself, you are not only telling the world your truth but also reinforcing it within your own mind, heightening the energetic charge as it takes shape through your voice. This practice is most effective when you look into your own eyes and connect deeply with the words you are saying.

In moments when anxiety threatens to overwhelm, a simple mantra can become your anchor. I was recently in an Uber on my way back home from a night out. It was late, and when I sat alone in the back seat, I immediately felt an eerie feeling—a sense of danger and unease. I called my mom, who stayed on the phone with me, reassuring and grounding me as I spoke to her in my native tongue, Portuguese. The driver knew I was on the phone and turned his podcast up louder. Then louder. Soon the podcast was blasting in the car, holding forth on war and death. It was aggressive and bizarre. I don't know if the situation was unsafe, but my body was on edge, in fight-or-flight mode, overwhelmed and sweating as I imagined the worst-case scenario. My mother was already on the phone if anything else happened, so I had covered my physical safety bases the best I could. But my continued panic was a sign I had no choice but to take seriously. As I sought grounding and calm, these words came to me:

"The world is vast, and I am safe."

"The world is vast, and I am safe."

I whispered this to myself over and over as we drove home. With each repetition, the grip of anxiety loosened, and I felt myself returning to a state of equilibrium. The chaos of the world faded into the background, and I was reminded of my own vastness too. Whatever impending disaster or strange energy that was in the air was stilled until it vanished. *I'm okay now*, I thought. In the stillness that followed, I felt a change in my state of being.

That mantra has since become a lifeline, a reminder that within the immensity of the ever-changing universe, there is space for peace and safety. I offer it for you to use as well, to guide you back to your center, where your true self resides, untouched by the storms outside. Repeat it and see how it suits you:

The world is vast, and I am safe.

The world is vast, and I am safe.

You can go much further with affirmations, joining them to spiritual mantras, singing and chanting them, in any style that resonates with your beliefs. You can join affirmations to prayer, since they are of similar alignment, intentionally speaking grace into being. It can be a moving experience to utter an affirmation or a mantra with fervor and ecstasy, while dancing or beating a drum, allowing the vibrations to rise and rise inside you as you feel your power rising too.

There is also the practice of repeating affirmations while tapping using the Emotional Freedom Technique, which was first developed by Gary Craig. Craig observed that repeated, gentle tapping on a sequence of acupressure points around the face, neck, chest, and near the lymph nodes under the arm helped regulate anxiety. He combined this with a method of crafting affirmations that roll out sequentially, as you tap through the different points. The first step is to acknowledge the discomfort or the trigger, and in the same thought, using not a "but" but an "and," repeating that you love and accept yourself deeply. Then, using the same approach as journal rewriting, you compose a narrative of new understanding around the trigger, ending up in a place of empowerment and agency.

Integrating shadow material is like working a muscle that gets stronger and surer the more you engage in a self-supportive routine. In this sense, ideally, you join both forms of integration I delineated above: the structured and intentional with the daily and the mundane.

Integrating shadow material is like working a muscle that gets stronger and surer the more you engage in a self-supportive routine.

"Every time I taught a client how to do shadow work, I taught them to meditate," says Connie Zweig. "That capacity to center yourself, connect to your breath, and feel grounded when meeting that scary part is really essential. I didn't impose any tradition on clients. Some people wanted a Christian mystical meditation, or a Jewish one, or Buddhist. But you get to know your mind when you're sitting. You're building a relationship with yourself, and your shadow. You learn to break your identification with it. 'I am not that, I am a soul on the journey.' When you start to make that shift, you realize you're not what you do, but that you have a spiritual nature. You let go of the success and the productivity and the doing and you come to a higher guidance that helps you get through the shadows."

As with all phases of shadow work, from start to restart, from investigating to processing, there must be an awareness of the body too. As part of her client aftercare, DeMartine always counsels regular mindful physical activity. "You can have those aha moments, but how can you connect to it all without it just being a disembodied concept?" she asks. "Rather than, 'Oh, this weird thing happened, and now, whoops, back to normal,' you incorporate some practical life skills every day so you're not just feeling like you're stuck in a black cloud."

Like with Zweig's meditation, what matters is the intention you bring to it, not the specific form. "There isn't one practice that works for everyone, because everybody integrates in their own way," says DeMartine. "I have some clients that really like to dance, so after sessions I'll tell them, 'Now put your favorite music on, blast it, and do whatever kind of dance you want.' One client I have is sixty, and she's just not going to get into Kundalini yoga, but I know she likes salsa." Dancing mindfully, in reflection on what she had been experiencing and how her perspective had been changing, anchored and grounded her progress.

Even as we come to recognize our shadows with love and compassion, they will always be with us. The shadow's contents may change as we change and evolve, and its disruptive intensity may calm, but the shadow itself never disappears. There will always be something in us we feel an urge to reject, always something swimming around inside us that doesn't want to be seen. This is simply part of being human. If you've read this far, I am quite sure you're now more curious than scared. Just keep going.

Benjamin Bernstein has a theory that he calls "the great onion of consciousness." He explains: "The premise is that each human has a higher self that created the human part. It's like a big ball of light, way more awake than the human part. And the reason the human isn't getting more of that higher self-consciousness is because around this big ball of light are all these dark onion layers, each of which is an unhealed wound or trauma. They might have come from this life, or maybe from a past life. If you do effective shadow work, you peel away the onion layers. Each layer you peel falls away, and more of the divine higher self is available to your human self. There's an automatic awakening that happens every time a good piece of shadow work is done."

Even if shadow work is never finished, in doing it you never return to the same place. If a tree loses its leaves every fall, it also grows bigger, stronger branches, reaching past itself continually, as long as there is life force left in it. The same is true with the growth and evolution that comes from shadow work. It is work. But it is work that brings astonishing rewards.

Shadow work is not a onetime challenge but an ongoing process of self-discovery and healing. Because of this, it is important for you to find that shadow flow—learning to dance with your shadows when they arise, knowing how to tend to them with care and compassion. Shadow flow is like a current of water that circulates and recirculates, returning to its source only to extend outward again. When you're not in a defensive crouch around what you learn, when the channels of communication are opened routinely, you develop a real relationship with yourself, one that is honest and nurturing.

Shadow work is not a onetime challenge but an ongoing process of self-discovery and healing.

You know you've found that flow when you learn to recognize your triggers and the emotional currents that come with them and start to see these moments not as disruptions but as chances to know yourself better. Each shadow that emerges is a teacher, showing you where healing is needed, where old wounds still linger, and that you can keep growing.

In this process, your past suffering becomes a tool to navigate future adversities. When your shadow makes itself felt, you know how to tend to it, how to soothe it and work with what you learn.

Meanwhile, if there is always the shadow, there is also always the light. Shadow work begins with awareness—the moment we become conscious of the unconscious. It's when we take a magnifying glass to our inner world, noticing the small, often hidden truths and half-truths that shape our lives. This is the foundation, the first step toward unraveling the stories we've been living by.

We trace newfound insights back to their origins, embarking on an expedition through the past. We review the experiences that have shaped us, connecting the dots to reveal the larger picture, seeing the patterns, the narratives we've been telling ourselves, and what they truly mean. Understanding transforms the chaos that once threatened to consume us into wisdom, guiding us forward with clarity and purpose.

Once you have gotten into that shadow flow and develop some familiarity with it, you are ready for light work, the ultimate form of living with the integrated shadow. Without practice, all that knowledge and wisdom can slip through your fingers like sand. It's reinforced by living out your strengths, awareness, and understanding to build a fortress of purpose and virtue, where you can navigate life with intention and integrity.

Where shadow work encourages us to uncover and accept our disavowed inner darkness so we can better integrate all of ourselves, light work cultivates and projects the aspects of our being that both serve our highest good and contribute positively to the collective. If shadow work is about introspection and healing the parts of ourselves that we often turn away from, light work is amplifying our inherent gifts, talents, and positive traits to outwardly express integrated wholeness to help heal the world.

We've seen examples of light work in this chapter and elsewhere in the book already. It is a subject that I think deserves more attention of its own, which is why *The Light Work Journal* is my next project and a natural follow-up to this book. Light work means putting an even greater emphasis on living out shadow work integration proactively, consciously using your voice to advocate for others, your creativity to inspire change, or your wisdom to guide those seeking direction. It is shining your inner light through acts of kindness, creativity, and leadership, inspiring others to do the same and creating a ripple effect that uplifts us all. It is a process of learning to give from a place of wholeness and to extend your intentions rooted in service to others; to manifest with a heart for humanity.

Life is interesting. In the end, some of your greatest pains become your greatest strengths, and when you feel buried, you are actually being planted. Your ability to contemplate and turn pain into wisdom is a rare and beautiful thing. Find peace within the patience required in this path and embrace the uncertainty with a soft smile. Enjoy the beauty of becoming.

I want to close with one last thought. I'm not here to fix you or tell you how to fix yourself. There's nothing to fix, because you're not really broken. What I'm here to do is plant a seed of peace. Tending to it is your work, your journey. I simply offer this beginning. This seed won't flourish overnight. It requires patience, attention, and care. Peace isn't a destination but a practice, a state of being that you return to again and again, standing in the calm center of your dark and light. And in that calm, you'll find the strength and clarity to navigate whatever life brings your way. You will learn to be a different kind of vulnerable—the strong kind of vulnerable. My role is simply to help you remember that this peace, this seed, this middle ground of infinite wisdom has always been within you, waiting to be awakened.

To live on a seesaw of duality,
Playing both weights,
Weighing both sides down,
With heavy thoughts,
And lighter laughs,
And heavy hearts,
And lighter loves,
This—
Is life.
Is us.

ACKNOWLEDGMENTS

To the many individuals who opened their hearts and stories to be part of this global conversation: thank you for your courage. You have gifted this book its breath and soul, making it a living testament to the power of shadow work.

To my husband, Abraham Shaheen, whose belief in me is as boundless as his kindness. Your steady support not only propels me forward, but uplifts all those fortunate enough to know you. Thank you for being my anchor and my light.

To my guide and lantern, Dr. Connie Zweig, whose open heart and unwavering wisdom cut through barriers, illuminating the path with knowledge and truth. Your guidance has been a source of both strength and clarity.

To my parents, Mamãe e Papai, who have set the most beautiful examples of goodness, virtue, and love. You have led me to the path of the soul, showing me the essence of integrity and the importance of inner work. I am forever grateful for your presence in my life.

To those journalers and readers of shadow work; to my agents, Albert Lee and Rebecca Gradinger, whose enthusiasm brought this work a new life and expansion. To Alexandra Marshall, whose insights and support enriched and shaped this work. To Michelle Herrera, visionary publisher who saw the spark in me and chose to foster the spirit of my work.

And to you. Boundless, infinite you. You, who have been pulled here now, whose intentional thoughts and actions will contribute to a more loving world. Together, may we continue to create a world grounded in love, understanding, and self-awareness.

NOTES

INTRODUCTION: HOW I GOT HERE

1. C. G. Jung, *The Collected Works of Carl Jung, Volume 17: The Development of Personality* (New York: Bollingen Series XX/Princeton University Press, 1958), paragraph 286.

2. C. G. Jung, *Man and His Symbols* (New York: Dell, 1968).

CHAPTER ONE: WHAT IS SHADOW WORK? HOW DO YOU START?

1. C. G. Jung, *The Collected Works of Carl Jung, Volume 17: The Development of Personality* (New York: Bollingen Series XX/Princeton University Press, 1958), paragraph 131.

2. Benjamin Bernstein, *Instant Divine Assistance: Your Complete Guide to Fast and Easy Spiritual Awakening, Healing and More* (Asheville, NC: Benjamin Bernstein, 2022).

CHAPTER TWO: A FIELD GUIDE TO THE EMOTIONS

1. C. G. Jung, *The Collected Works of Carl Jung, Volume 6: Psychological Types* (New York: Bollingen Series XX/Princeton University Press, 1971), paragraph 856.

2. Peter Levine, *An Autobiography of Trauma: A Healing Journey* (Rochester, VT: Park Street Press, 2024).

3. Interview with Guy Macpherson, *The Trauma Therapist* podcast (The Trauma Therapist Project), Episode 810, March 18, 2024.

4. Bessel van der Kolk, *The Body Keeps the Score: Mind, Brain and Body in the Transformation of Trauma* (New York: Penguin, 2014), 56.

5. Peter Levine, *In an Unspoken Voice: How the Body Releases Trauma and Restores Goodness* (Berkeley, CA: North Atlantic Books, 2010).

6. Ibid., 16.

7. Ibid., 17.

CHAPTER THREE: SHADOW WORK AND SPIRITUALITY

1. C. G. Jung, *Modern Man in Search of a Soul* (Boston, MA: Mariner Books Classics, 1955).

2. C. G. Jung, *Memories, Dreams, Reflections* (London: Williams Collins, 1961), 380–81.

3. C. G. Jung et al., *Man and His Symbols* (New York: Dell, 1968), 84.

4. C. G. Jung, *Memories, Dreams, Reflections* (London: Williams Collins, 1961).

5. Rainn Wilson, *Soul Boom: Why We Need a Spiritual Revolution* (New York: Hachette, New 2023).

6. Richard Schwartz, *No Bad Parts: Healing Trauma and Restoring Wholeness with the Internal Family Systems Model* (Boulder, CO: Sounds True, 2021).

7. Ibid., 3.

8. Lea Suruge, "Why This Paleolithic Burial Site Is So Strange (and So Important)," Sapiens.org, February 22, 2018, https://www.sapiens.org/archaeology/paleolithic-burial-sunghir/.

9. Ryan Z. Cortazar, "Scholar: Cave Paintings Show Religious Sophistication," *Harvard Gazette*, April 26, 2007, https://news.harvard.edu/gazette/story/2007/04/scholar-cave-paintings-show-religious-sophistication/.

10. C. Michael Smith, *Jung and Shamanism in Dialogue: Retrieving the Soul, Retrieving the Sacred* (Bloomington, IN: Trafford, 2007), 1.

11. Ibid., 64.

12. C. G. Jung, *Memories, Dreams, Reflections* (London: Williams Collins, 1961), 387.

13. C. G. Jung, *The Collected Works of Carl Jung, Volume 9, Part 1: The Archetypes and the Collective Unconscious* (New York: Bollingen Series XX/Princeton University Press, 1959), 58.

14. Rupert Sheldrake, *The Presence of the Past: Morphic Resonance and the Memory of Nature* (Rochester, VT: Park Street Press, 2012).

15. Robert Amacker, "The Reluctant Shaman Returns," bobamacker.com/shamanic-adventures/the-reluctant-shaman/.

16. Dennis Merritt, "Reflections on Thirty-Six Years of Participation in Lakota Sioux Sweat Lodge Ceremonies," *Ecopsychology* 15, no. 3 (September 19, 2023).

17. Ibid.

18. Benjamin Bernstein, *Instant Divine Assistance: Your Complete Guide to Fast and Easy Spiritual Awakening, Healing and More* (Asheville, NC: Benjamin Bernstein, 2022).

CHAPTER FOUR: A CALL TO QUEST

1. John G. Neihardt, *Black Elk Speaks: Being the Life Story of a Holy Man of the Oglala Sioux* (Winnipeg, MB: Bison Books, 2014), 53.

2. Carol S. Pearson, *Awakening the Heroes Within: Twelve Archetypes to Help Us Find Ourselves and Transform Our World* (New York: HarperCollins, 1991), 18.

3. John Rowan, "Using Archetypes in Therapy," *Thresholds* (Spring 2016), bacp.co.uk/bacp-journals/thresholds/spring-2016/archetypes-in-therapy/.

4. Jay Earley, *Self-Therapy: A Step-by-Step Guide to Creating Wholeness Using IFS, a Cutting-Edge Psychotherapy* (San Rafael, CA: Pattern Systems Books, 2022), 93.

5. Dennis Merritt, "Use of the *I Ching* in the Analytic Setting," *Junganthology* (October 21, 2020), https://jungchicago.org/blog/dennis-merritt-use-of-the-i-ching-in-the-analytic-setting/.

CHAPTER FIVE: THE SHADOW IN INTIMACY

1. C. G. Jung, *Letters, Volume 1: 1906–1950*, ed. Gerhard Adler with Aniela Jaffé (London: Routledge, 1953), 237.

2. Connie Zweig, *Romancing the Shadow: A Guide to Soul Work for a Vital, Authentic Life* (Wellspring/Ballantine).

3. C. G. Jung, *Memories, Dreams, Reflections* (London: Williams Collins, 1961), 293.

4. Resmaa Menakem, *Monsters in Love: Why Your Partner Sometimes Drives You Crazy—and What You Can Do About It* (Central Recovery Press), Kindle Edition, placement 459/5750.

5. Ibid.

6. *Monsters in Love*, Kindle Edition, placement 1012/5750.

7. C. G. Jung, *The Collected Works of Carl Jung, Volume 7: Two Essays in Analytical Psychology* (New York: Bollingen Series XX/Princeton University Press, 1953), paragraph 78.

CHAPTER SIX: THE SOCIAL SHADOW

1. Interview with Krista Tippett, *On Being*, podcast, April 12, 2021, https://www.youtube.com/watch?v=ADxoo2Xae-Y.

2. C. G. Jung, *The Collected Works of Carl Jung, Volume 9 Part II: Aion: Researches into the Phenomenology of Self* (New York: Bollingen Series XX/ Princeton University Press, 1959), paragraph 17.

3. "Epigenetics and Child Development: How Children's Experiences Affect Their Genes," Center on the Developing Child, Harvard University, developingchild.harvard.edu/resources/ what-is-epigenetics-and-how-does-it-relate-to-child-development/.

4. Resmaa Menakem, *My Grandmother's Hands: Racialized Trauma and the Pathway to Mending Our Hearts and Bodies* (Las Vegas: Central Recovery Press, 2017), Kindle Edition, placement 331.

5. Ibid., Kindle edition, placement 345.

6. Jelly Roll, "Save Me," *Whitsitt Chapel* (BBR Music Group), https:// www.youtube.com/watch?v=FxFNprPOdss.

7. Jelly Roll, "Save Me," ABC News Studios, May 30, 2023.

8. *Daily Show*, Comedy Central, December 8, 2023, https://www.you tube.com/watch?v=J7rE4V8rNtw.

9. Connie Zweig and Jeremiah Abrams, eds., *Meeting the Shadow: The Hidden Power of the Dark Side of Human Nature* (New York: TarcherPerigee, 2020).

10. C. G. Jung, *The Collected Works of Carl Jung, Volume 10: The Undiscovered Self* (New York: Bollingen Series XX/Princeton University Press, 1957), 12–13.

11. Ibid., 24.

12. Partrick Kanyangara, Bernard Rimé, Dario Paez, and Vincent Yzerbyt, "Trust, Individual Guilt, Collective Guilt and Dispositions Toward Reconciliation Among Rwandan Survivors and Prisoners Before and After Their Participation in Postgenocide Gacaca Courts in Rwanda," *Journal of Social and Political Psychology* (August 7, 2014).

13. Pumla Godobo-Madikizela, "Why Do We Fear Forgiveness," *New York Times*, June 17, 2024, https://www.nytimes.com/2024/06/17/special-series/ south-africa-apartheid-forgiveness-fear.html?searchResultPosition=6.

14. Thich Nhat Hanh, Closing remarks of the Day of Mindfulness at Spirit Rock Center in Woodacre, California, October 1993, https://inquir ingmind.com/article/1002_41_thich-nhat_hanh/.

15. Emily Cutts, *The Dear Wild Place: Green Spaces, Community and Campaigning* (Paisley, UK: CCWB Press, 2019).

16. Ibid., 23.

17. Sunny Fitzgerald, "The Secret to Mindful Travel? A Walk in the Woods," *National Geographic*, October 18, 2019.

18. *The Dear Wild Place: Green Spaces, Community and Campaigning*, 14.

19. Ibid., 86.

20. Ibid, 95.

CHAPTER SEVEN: THE TECHNOLOGICAL SHADOW

1. Virginia Heffernan, *Magic and Loss: The Internet as Art* (New York: Simon & Schuster, 2017), 241.

2. Paul Virilio and Philippe Petit, *Politics of the Very Worst: Semiotext(e)* (Cambridge, MA: MIT Press, 1999), 89.

3. C. G. Jung, *The Collected Works of Carl Jung, Volume 18: The Symbolic Life: Miscellaneous Writings* (New York: Bollingen Series XX/Princeton University Press, 1950), paragraph 1407.

4. Kara Swisher, *Burn Book: A Tech Love Story* (New York: Simon & Schuster, 2024), excerpted in *Washington Post*, February 13, 2024.

5. *Magic and Loss: The Internet as Art*, 10–11.

6. "Screen Use Disrupts Precious Sleep Time," National Sleep Foundation, March 13, 2022, https://www.thensf.org/screen-use-disrupts-precious-sleep-time/.

7. Patience Waite, "Senate Hearing Tackles Harms Caused by Social Media Algorithms," Nextgov.com, December 13, 2021, https://www.nextgov.com/policy/2021/12/senate-hearing-tackles-harms-caused-social-media-algorithms/359700/.

8. Jonathan Stray, Ravi Iyer, and Helena Puig Laurrari, "The Algorithmic Management of Polarization and Violence on Social Media," Knight First Amendment Institute at Columbia University, August 22, 2023, https://knightcolumbia.org/content/the-algorithmic-management-of-polarization-and-violence-on-social-media.

9. Kara Swisher, "The Expensive Education of Mark Zuckerberg and Silicon Valley," *New York Times*, February 8, 2018, https://www.nytimes.com/2018/08/02/opinion/the-expensive-education-of-mark-zuckerberg-and-silicon-valley.html.

10. Lien Faelens, Kristof Hoorelbeke, Ruben Cambier, et al., "The Relationship between Instagram Use and Indicators of Mental Health: A Systematic Review," *Science Direct* 4 (August–December 2021), https://www.sciencedirect.com/science/article/pii/S2451958821000695#appsec1.

11. Chelsea P. Butkowski, Travis L. Dixon, and Kristopher Weeks, "Body Surveillance on Instagram: Examining the Role of Selfie Feedback Investment in Young Adult Women's Body Image Concerns," *Sex Roles, a Journal of Research* 81 (January 5, 2019).

12. Nick Bilton, "Steve Jobs Was a Low-Tech Parent," *New York Times*, September 10, 2014, https://www.nytimes.com/2014/09/11/fashion/steve-jobs-apple-was-a-low-tech-parent.html.

13. Tik Root, "What Happens When a School Bans Smartphones? A Complete Transformation," *The Guardian*, January 17, 2024, https://www.theguardian.com/lifeandstyle/2024/jan/17/cellphone-smartphone-bans-schools.

14. "Our Epidemic of Loneliness and Isolation: The US Surgeon General's Advisory on the Healing Effects of Social Connection and Community," 2023, chrome-extension://efaidnbmnnnibpcajpC.G.lclefindmkaj/https://www.hhs.gov/sites/default/files/surgeon-general-social-connection-advisory.pdf.

15. Ibid.

16. Richard Morris, "Researchers Warn of Rise in Extremism Online after Covid," BBC News, December 30, 2022, https://www.bbc.com/news/uk-politics-61106191.

17. Alice Marwick, Benjamin Clancy, and Katherine Furl, "Far Right Online Radicalization: A Review of the Literature," *Bulletin of Technology and Public Life,* University of North Carolina at Chapel Hill, May 10, 2022, https://citap.pubpub.org/pub/jq7l6jny/release/1.

18. Thomas Davenport and Ravi Kalakota, "The Potential for Artificial Intelligence in Health Care," *Future Healthcare Journal* (June 2019).

19. Nitasha Tiku, Kevin Schaul, and Szu Yu Chen, "These Fake Images Reveal how AI Amplifies Our Worst Stereotypes," *Washington Post*, November 1, 2023, https://www.washingtonpost.com/technology/interactive/2023/ai-generated-images-bias-racism-sexism-stereotypes/.

CHAPTER EIGHT: INTEGRATING THE SHADOW

1. C. G. Jung, *The Collected Works of Carl Jung, Volume 18: The Symbolic Life: Miscellaneous Writings* (New York: Bollingen Series XX/Princeton University Press, 1950), paragraph 1703.

2. Ibid, paragraph 1402.

3. Richard Tedeschi, "Growth After Trauma," *Harvard Business Review*, July–August 2020, https://hbr.org/2020/07/growth-after-trauma.

4. Stephen Joseph, *What Doesn't Kill Us: The New Psychology of Post-Traumatic Growth* (New York: Basic Books, 2013).

5. Stephen Joseph, "What Doesn't Kill Us . . . ," *The Psychologist* (British Psychological Society), November 26, 2012, https://www.bps.org.uk/psychologist/what-doesnt-kill-us.

6. Lois Beckett, "Fred Guttenberg Will Not Sit Down: Florida Father Demands Gun Reform," *The Guardian*, March 11, 2018, https://www.theguardian.com/us-news/2018/mar/11/after-losing-his-daughter-florida-father-demands-gun-reform-im-not-going-away?subid=21785878&CMP=GT_US_collection.

7. Michaela Haas, *Bouncing Forward: Transforming Bad Breaks into Breakthroughs* (New York: Simon & Schuster, 2015).

8. Soraya Chemaly, *The Resilience Myth: New Thinking on Grit, Strength, and Growth After Trauma* (New York: Simon & Schuster, 2024), 186.

ABOUT THE AUTHOR

Keila Shaheen is the creator of Zenfulnote and author of the viral sensation *The Shadow Work Journal*. A certified sound healer and behavioral therapy practitioner, she founded Zenfulnote in 2021 to provide innovative tools for inner healing. Her work has been featured in the *New York Times*, *Billboard*, and the *Atlantic*. Keila is also a flutist and musical artist, creating music to inspire peace on the planet, and a NAMI ambassador, committed to making mental wellness accessible and welcoming for everyone.

www.zenfulnote.com